ALSO FROM UK DRIVING

LEARNING TO DRIVE:

Teaching a Learner Driver –
A Guide for Amateur Instructors
Learning to Drive –
The Learner Driver's Manual
Teach Yourself Traffic Signs
& Road Markings
The Learner Driver's Logbook –
Lesson Plan & Progress Record
The Driving Test & How to Pass –
An Examiner's Guide to the 'L' Test

250 THEORY TEST QUESTIONS:

Cars - Motorcycles - LGV - PCV - ADI

HIGHWAY CODE & THEORY TEST QUESTIONS:

Cars - Motorcycles - LGV - PCV - ADI

The Highway Code
How to Drive on a Motorway
Driving at Night & in Bad Weather

All available from www.ukdrivingskills.co.uk

250 Theory Test Practise Questions for ADIs

UK Driving Skills
Theory Test Question Series

Don L. Gates

www.ukdrivingskills.co.uk

250 Theory Test Practise Questions for ADIs

This product includes the Driver and Vehicle Standards Agency (DVSA) revision question bank.

The Driver and Vehicle Standards Agency (DVSA) has given permission for the reproduction of Crown copyright material. DVSA does not accept responsibility for the accuracy of the reproduction.

Contents

About the Theory Test

In order to take a theory test, you must have lived in England, Wales or Scotland for at least 185 days in the last 12 months before the day you sit your test.

You can book your approved driving instructor (ADI) part 1 test when your application to start the ADI qualifying process has been accepted.

You must pass your theory test before you can take the part 2 practical driving test.

What to Take With You

You must take your UK photo card driving licence to your test. If you have a licence from Northern Ireland, take the photo card and paper counterpart licence. Your test will be cancelled and you will lose your fee if you do not take the correct things with you.

If you have an old style paper licence you must also take a valid passport for photo ID. If you do not have a passport, you need to get a photo card licence.

You will need to show your licence or ID to the staff when you arrive at the test centre. There will also be security checks to make sure that you're not carrying anything which could enable you to contact anyone outside of the test centre.

If you have any personal possessions, you must put these in a secure locker or place them under your desk in a bag which staff will provide. It's best to take nothing with you that you don't really need.

Starting the Test

A member of staff will take you to a room where other candidates will be sat in cubicles also taking the test. You must be quiet but don't be afraid to ask questions.

The test is fairly straightforward and all the instructions will be shown on the screen in front of you. If you wish you can choose to have a practise session to get used to the way the test works.

Multiple Choice Questions

Once you begin the test, you will have 90 minutes to answer 100 questions. You need to score at least 85 points to pass, and at least 20 out of 25 points in each of the 4 categories of questions:

- road procedure
- traffic signs and signals, car control, pedestrians and mechanical knowledge
- driving test, disabilities, and the law
- publications and instructional techniques.

Hazard Perception

You may take a 3 minute break if you wish before starting the second part of the test. When you're ready, you should put on the provided headphones to watch an explanatory video of the hazard perception element.

You will be shown 14 video clips during which you need to click the mouse when you see a 'developing hazard', such as a vehicle about to emerge from a junction or a pedestrian about to step off the kerb; something which would cause you as a driver to alter speed or direction.

Click at the right time to score a maximum of 5 points for each clip. Don't just click randomly as you may be penalised for clicking too many times. One of the clips will have 2 hazards for you to identify. There is a maximum of 75 points and you need a minimum of 57 points to pass.

Test Result

You will get your test result shortly after finishing. You need to reach the minimum score in both parts to pass.

If you're not successful you must wait at least 3 working days before you can try again. If you pass, you will need to use your pass certificate number in order to go ahead and book your practical driving test. The certificate is valid for 2 years. If you haven't passed your driving test within this time you will need to sit the theory test again.

Book a Theory Test

When you're ready to take a theory test, you can either:

- call the central booking line on 0300 200 11 22
- use the online booking system at - https://www.gov.uk/book-theory-test (easiest)

Before booking make sure that you have your:

- UK driving licence number
- an email address
- credit or debit card for payment
- your personal reference number issued by the DVSA

Special Needs

If you have any special needs you must mention this at the time of booking. Where possible, the theory test centre may be able to make adjustments to help you overcome any difficulties you may have.

About this Book

The material in this book is reproduced under licence from the Driver & Vehicle Standards Agency.

Questions are based on the official DVSA theory test question revision bank. They are designed to help you revise and practise for your theory test.

Questions marked with an asterisk* are not from the DVSA question bank and are © Copyright UK Driving Skills

Whilst every care is taken to ensure the accuracy of these questions and answers, if you do spot any errors please contact UK Driving Skills via our website to bring these to our attention.

About the Questions

Each practise set consists of 50 multiple choice questions. Mark the letter to the left of each answer you think is correct.

You will find the correct answers over the page; you will also be given an explanation of the answer helping to reinforce your knowledge on the subject.

Test One

Question 1

Your pupil asks you about towing a trailer after they have passed their driving test. What should you tell them to do?

A   Ask DVLA to update their licence

B   Take professional training

C   Fit P plates to the trailer

D   To take a special driving test

Question 2 *

What does this sign mean?

A   Warning of school children

B   Zebra crossing ahead

C   Pedestrians walking along the road

D   Pedestrians prohibited

Answers

Question 1

B - They need to know how to tow a trailer safely. This includes hitching the trailer to the vehicle, checking the trailer for defects, reversing with a trailer and how to deal with any problems. There are accredited trainers who can teach them these skills. Professional training will also give them confidence in their ability to tow a trailer safely.

Question 2

C - You will sometimes see this sign where there are no footpaths; you may encounter people walking along the edges of the road.

Question 3 *

As you are driving along, you see a long vehicle starting to emerge from a junction on your right. The driver is about to swing into your path. What should you tell your pupil to do?

A   Reduce speed and allow the driver to emerge

B   Maintain your speed as you have right of way

C   Warn the driver by flashing your lights

D   Mount the pavement to avoid it

Question 4

A group of horse riders comes towards you. What should you do if the leading rider's horse becomes nervous of your presence?

A   Increase speed to pass the riders quickly

B   Continue driving carefully and keep well to the left

C   Brake to a stop as quickly as possible

D   Brake gently to a stop until they have passed

Question 5

What should you do if you see a large box fall from a lorry onto the motorway?

A   Go to the next emergency telephone and report the hazard

B   Catch up with the lorry and try to get the driver's attention

C   Stop near to the box until the police arrive

D   Pull over to the hard shoulder, then remove the box

Answers

Question 3

A - Drivers of long vehicles sometimes need to swing wide so that their trailers don't cut in across the pavement, and they won't be able to pull out and clear the junction as quickly as a car driver would. To be safe, you need to slow down and give the driver time.

Question 4

D - If any animal you pass on the road becomes unsettled, you should brake gently to avoid startling them and come to a stop. A nervous animal is unpredictable, so you should wait until it has settled or passed by.

Question 5

A - Lorry drivers can be unaware of objects falling from their vehicles. If you see something fall onto a motorway, look to see if the driver pulls over. If they don't stop, don't attempt to retrieve the object yourself. Pull onto the hard shoulder near an emergency telephone and report the hazard.

Question 6 *

You are teaching your pupil how to reverse a car into a side road on the left. What should you teach them to do if the rear nearside tyre touches the kerb?

A   Drive around the corner to where they started from and start again

B   Accept that they are not ready for this exercise and drive off

C   Keep going backwards until they mount the kerb and then pull forward

D   Drive forward to straighten the car and then continue reversing

Question 7

How can you reduce the environmental harm caused by your motor vehicle?

A   Only use it for short journeys

B   Don't service it so often

C   Avoid driving too slowly

D   Reduce the amount of acceleration

Answers

Question 6

D - Just touching the kerb is not a serious error. The right course of action is to correct the mistake by pulling forward to adjust the position before a serious loss of control occurs.

Question 7

D - Engines that burn fossil fuels produce exhaust emissions that are harmful to health. The harder you make the engine work, the more emissions it will produce. Engines also use more fuel and produce higher levels of emissions when they're cold. Anything you can do to reduce your use of fossil fuels will help the environment.

Question 8

What is the main hazard you would need to make your pupil aware of as you approach this scene?

A   Vehicles turning right

B   Vehicles doing a U-turn

C   The cyclist waiting on the grass

D   Parked cars around the corner

Question 9 *

Anti-lock brakes are designed to help prevent you from skidding. When is this likely to be least effective?

A   When it is foggy

B   When the weather is cold

C   When the road surface is loose

D   When the tarmac is fresh

Answers

Question 8

C - The cyclist appears to be trying to cross the road. You must be able to deal with the unexpected, especially when you're approaching a hazardous junction. A driver needs to look well ahead to give themselves time to deal with any hazards An instructor needs to look even further ahead to allow time for instruction and to make allowances for a novice's slow reactions or errors.

Question 9

C - There will be little for your tyres to grip onto when the road surface is loose or damaged. In this situation anti-lock braking may not be of much help.

Question 10

You park at night on a road with a 40 mph speed limit. What should you do?

A   Park facing the traffic

B   Leave parking lights on

C   Leave dipped headlights on

D   Park near a street light

Question 11 *

You are approaching a busy junction. You have asked your pupil to continue ahead. At the last moment they realise that they are in a lane marked for turning left. What should you tell them to do?

A   To stay in that lane and turn left

B   To stop until the junction clears

C   To signal right and start looking over their shoulder

D   To start edging over until someone gives way

Question 12

What can a loose filler cap on your diesel fuel tank cause?

A   It can make the engine difficult to start

B   It can make the roads slippery for other road users

C   It can increase your vehicle's fuel consumption

D   It can increase the level of exhaust emissions

Answers

Question 10

B - You must use parking lights when parking at night on a road or in a lay-by on a road with a speed limit greater than 30 mph. You must also park in the direction of the traffic flow and not close to a junction.

Question 11

A - If there is not time for a safe change of lanes then it should not be attempted. Teach your pupil to follow the road markings rather than cause problems for other drivers. You can always use another way if you need to get back on route.

Question 12

B - Diesel fuel can spill out if your filler cap isn't secured properly. This is most likely to occur on bends, junctions and roundabouts, where it will make the road slippery, especially if it's wet. At the end of a dry spell of weather, the road surfaces may have a high level of diesel spillage that hasn't been washed away by rain.

Question 13

A single carriageway road has this sign. What's the maximum permitted speed for a car towing a trailer?

A   30 mph

B   40 mph

C   50 mph

D   60 mph

Question 14

When must your vehicle have valid insurance cover?

A   Before you can make a SORN

B   Before you can sell the vehicle

C   Before you can tax the vehicle

D   Before you can scrap the vehicle

Answers

Question 13

C - When you're towing a trailer, a reduced speed limit also applies on dual carriageways and motorways. These lower speed limits apply to vehicles pulling all sorts of trailers, including caravans and horse boxes.

Question 14

C - Your vehicle must have valid insurance cover before you can tax it. If required, it will also need to have a valid MOT certificate. You can tax your vehicle online, by phone or at certain post offices.

Question 15

For how long does a driving test pass certificate remain valid?

A 1 year

B 2 years

C 3 years

D 5 years

Question 16

How would it be illegal for a provisional licence holder to drive?

A At more than 40 mph

B With passengers in the rear seats

C Without an accompanying driver

D If they're under 18 years old

Answers

Question 15

B - When a candidate passes a practical driving test, their full licence is normally issued directly by the licensing authority. However, if this doesn't happen, successful candidates should apply for a full licence as soon as possible. The driving test pass certificate is valid for two years; if a full licence isn't applied for within that time, the driver will need to retake their test.

Question 16

C - When driving a motor car, a learner driver who holds a provisional driving licence must

- display red L plates (or D plates in Wales) to the front and rear of the vehicle
- be insured to drive the vehicle
- be accompanied by someone who's at least 21 years old and who has held for at least three years (and still holds) a full licence for the category of vehicle being driven

Question 17 *

You are driving on a road that has continuous double white lines along the centre of the road. When may you cross these lines to overtake?

A   When passing a car that is slowing down to turn left

B   When passing a vehicle that is travelling at less than 10 mph

C   When passing traffic that is queuing at a junction

D   When you can see that the right-hand side of the road is clear

Question 18 *

Which of these vehicles are not allowed to use the right-hand lane of a three-lane motorway?

A   Motorcycles fitted with a sidecar

B   Those which are towing a caravan

C   Cars driven by learner drivers

D   Any type of commercial vehicle

Answers

Question 17

B - If there are double white lines along the centre of the road and the line nearest you is continuous, you must not cross or straddle the line, except in specific circumstances. These include overtaking a slow moving vehicle which is travelling at less than10 mph.

Question 18

B - Vehicles towing a trailer are subject to lower speed limits. When a motorway has more than two lanes, a vehicle towing any kind of a trailer must not use the right hand lane.

Question 19 *

Windscreens have pillars which can partially restrict your view. When is this most likely to be a problem?

A   When there is oncoming traffic

B   When you are driving at higher speeds

C   When someone is following you

D   When you are turning at a junction

Question 20

What kind of pass certificate will the examiner issue if a disabled driver passes their test in a specially adapted car?

A   A pass certificate that states they can only drive a car with automatic transmission

B   A pass certificate that limits them to driving a suitably adapted car

C   A pass certificate that limits them to certain speed limits for three years

D   A pass certificate that's unrestricted

Question 21

When should you inflate your tyres to more than their normal pressure?

A   When the roads are slippery

B   When the vehicle is fitted with anti-lock brakes

C   When the tyre tread is worn below 2 mm

D   When carrying a heavy load

Answers

Question 19

D - When approaching bend and junctions, you need to look to the sides to widen your view, or to look for others before emerging. It is when turning your head that the door pillars may obstruct your view and these can easily hide pedestrians and those on two wheels.

Question 20

B - If a disabled driver passes their driving test in a specifically adapted motor car, the driving licence issued will restrict them to driving vehicles fitted with the same necessary adaptations.

Question 21

D - Check the vehicle handbook. This should give you guidance on the correct tyre pressures for your vehicle and when you may need to adjust them. If you're carrying a heavy load, you may need to adjust the headlights as well. Most cars have a switch on the dashboard to do this.

Question 22

What does the white line along the side of the road indicate?

A   The edge of the carriageway

B   The approach to a hazard

C   No parking

D   No overtaking

Question 23 *

A driver emerges from a junction ahead of you. You have to brake to avoid them. What should you do next?

A   Pull back and keep your distance

B   Follow closely to make them aware of your presence

C   Warn them with a flash of your lights

D   Overtake them immediately

Answers

Question 22

A - A continuous white line is used on many roads to indicate the edge of the carriageway. This can be useful when visibility is restricted. The line is discontinued at junctions, lay-bys, and entrances to or exits from private drives.

Question 23

A - There are many inconsiderate drivers on our roads, or the driver may be new and lacking in judgement. It's not easy, but if you can remain calm and ignore the error, you will remain a better and more focussed driver.

Question 24

What can happen if your car's wheels are unbalanced?

A   The steering will pull to one side

B   The steering wheel will vibrate

C   The brakes will be less effective

D   The steering will become heavy

Question 25

You are turning left into a side road. What hazard should you be especially aware of?

A   A change in speed limit

B   Pedestrians

C   Traffic congestion

D   Parked vehicles

Question 26

A driver is convicted of drinking and driving twice within 10 years. They wish to have their licence returned. Who do they have to satisfy that they do not have an alcohol problem?

A   The Driver and Vehicle Licensing Agency

B   The Driver and Vehicle Standards Agency

C   The Highways Agency

D   The Disclosure and Barring Service

Answers

Question 24

B - If your wheels are out of balance, it will cause the steering to vibrate at certain speeds. This isn't a fault that will put itself right, so take your vehicle to a garage or tyre fitter to have the wheels rebalanced.

Question 25

B - You must give way to any pedestrians who are crossing a road you are turning into. When it's safe, you should also give way to pedestrians who are waiting to step out. The 'Hierarchy of Road Users' gives pedestrians priority at junctions and you should always look into a side road and be ready to give way.

Question 26

A - You must be medically fit to drive. All issues relating to alcohol, drugs or health have to be reported to the DVLA Drivers Medical Group or, in Northern Ireland, the DVA Drivers Medical Section. If a licence is revoked for any health-related reason, you must reapply to the relevant medical branch and satisfy them that you're now fit to drive before they'll issue the appropriate licence for the category you require.

Question 27

What does this sign mean?

A   Give way to oncoming vehicles

B   Approaching traffic passes you on both sides

C   Turn off at the next available junction

D   Pass on either side

Question 28

What is the purpose of the green area marked on the road in this picture?

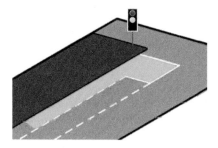

A   To allow room for pedestrians to cross the road

B   To allow space for large vehicles to turn

C   To allow cyclists to position in front of other traffic

D   To allow you to overshoot the stop line

Answers

Question 27

D - These signs are seen in one-way streets that have more than one lane. When you see this sign, use the route that's the most convenient and doesn't require a late change of direction.

Question 28

C - Advanced stop lines allow cyclists to take a position ahead of other traffic. When the green signal shows, they then have the time and space to move off in front of the following traffic.

Question 29

Your vehicle has a puncture on a motorway. What should you do?

A Drive slowly to the next service area to get assistance

B Pull up on the hard shoulder. Change the wheel as quickly as possible

C Pull up on the hard shoulder. Use the emergency phone to get assistance

D Switch on your hazard warning lights. Stop in your lane

Question 30

How will a convex mirror affect the appearance of following vehicles?

A They will seem to be closer

B They will seem to be further away

C They will seem to be clearer

D They will seem to be driving faster

Answers

Question 29

C - Pull up on the hard shoulder and make your way to the nearest emergency telephone to call for assistance. Don't attempt to repair your vehicle while it's on the hard shoulder, because of the risk posed by traffic passing at high speeds.

Question 30

B - Exterior mirrors are designed to be convex. This gives a wide angle of view and helps to reduce blind areas. However, a vehicle behind will appear smaller and further away in a convex mirror, so it could be closer than you think.

Question 31

What must you do at this junction?

A   Stop behind the line, then edge forward to see clearly

B   Stop beyond the line, at a point where you can see clearly

C   Stop only if there is traffic on the main road

D   Stop only if you are turning to the left

Question 32

You're on a motorway at night. In which situation may you have your headlights switched off?

A   When there are vehicles close in front of you

B   When you are travelling below 50 mph

C   When the motorway is brightly lit

D   When your vehicle is broken down on the hard shoulder

Answers

Question 31

A - The 'stop' sign has been put here because the view into the main road is poor. You must stop because it won't be possible to take proper observation while you're moving.

Question 32

D - Always use your headlights at night on a motorway, unless you've had to stop on the hard shoulder. If you have to use the hard shoulder, switch off your headlights but leave your parking lights on, so that your vehicle can be seen by other road users.

Question 33

What should you do when teaching a profoundly deaf pupil?

A Learn sign language to give instructions

B Write down all the directions for the route

C Ask the pupil how they would like you to communicate with them

D Give instructions slowly and distinctly while stationary

Question 34 *

What should you do if a driver coming up behind dazzles you with their lights at night?

A Use the anti-dazzle position for your mirror

B Avoid using your mirrors at night

C Brake regularly to flash your brake lights

D Switch on your main beam headlights

Answers

Question 33

C - Most people with hearing difficulties will have developed communications strategies that work for them. For example, they may be able to use a simple system of hand signals. However, if you're unable to work out a way of communicating effectively, you should consider referring the pupil to another driving instructor who has the necessary skills.

Question 34

A - Rear view mirrors have a small clip on the bottom edge, which will tilt the mirror and prevent you from being dazzled. You can click this back when the problem has gone away. Many modern cars now have automatically dipping mirrors.

Question 35

What does this sign mean?

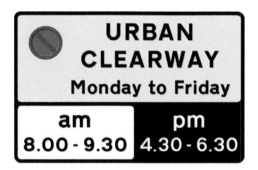

A   You can park on the days and times shown

B   No parking at all from Monday to Friday

C   No parking on the days and times shown

D   End of the urban clearway restrictions

Question 36

On a road where trams operate, which of these vehicles will be most at risk from the tram rails?

A   Cars

B   Cycles

C   Buses

D   Lorries

Answers

Question 35

C - Urban clearways are provided to keep traffic flowing at busy times. You may stop only briefly to set down or pick up passengers. Times of operation will vary from place to place, so always check the signs.

Question 36

B - The narrow wheels of a bicycle can become stuck in the tram rails, causing the cyclist to stop suddenly, wobble or even lose balance altogether. The tram lines are also slippery, which could cause a cyclist to slide or fall off. Make sure that you teach your pupils to allow riders plenty of room in these situations.

Question 37

What information is found on a vehicle registration document?

A   The registered keeper

B   The type of insurance cover

C   The service history details

D   The date of the MOT

Question 38 *

How does a toucan crossing differ from other types of crossing?

A   Horse riders can also use it

B   Traffic wardens control it

C   It only operates at peak times

D   Cyclists can also use it

Question 39

Where can you find reflective amber studs on a motorway?

A   Separating the slip road from the motorway

B   On the left-hand edge of the road

C   On the right-hand edge of the road

D   Separating the lanes

Answers

Question 37

A - Every vehicle used on the road has a registration document. This shows the vehicle's details, including date of first registration, registration number, registered keeper, previous keeper, make of vehicle, engine size, chassis number, year of manufacture and colour.

Question 38

D - Toucan crossings are shared by pedestrians and cyclists, who are allowed to ride across. Unlike the pelican crossing there is no flashing amber phase, the light sequence is the same as normal traffic lights.

Question 39

C - At night or in poor visibility, reflective studs on the road help you to judge your position on the carriageway. Amber studs mark the edge of the central reservation.

Question 40 *

A pupil fails their driving test but disagrees with the examiner's decision and wants to get the result overturned. What do you tell them to do?

A   Write to the test centre to complain

B   Tell them that the result of a test cannot be changed

C   Go to the centre to talk to the examiner

D   Tell them to write to the DVSA head office

Question 41 *

Which sign means that pedestrians are not allowed?

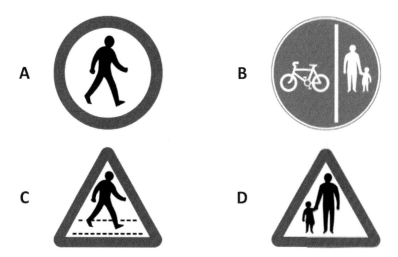

A

B

C

D

Answers

Question 40

B - Nervous candidates are sometimes completely unaware of the mistakes they make during a driving test, even when the examiner explains they may still not recall the situation. They also sometimes just don't realise that what they have done is considered a serious fault. It always helps if the instructor is there at the end to listen to the debrief. The result of a test cannot be overturned however, even in a court of law.

Question 41

A - There are a number of different signs showing pedestrians but each one has a different meaning. It is important that you know what each one means and that this knowledge is passed on to those you teach.

Question 42

When will you feel the effects of engine braking?

A   When you change from forward to reverse gear

B   When you are in neutral

C   When you change to a lower gear

D   When you change to a higher gear

Question 43

You are driving on a wet road. You have to stop your vehicle in an emergency to avoid a pedestrian. What should you teach your pupil to do?

A   Apply both the handbrake and footbrake

B   Keep both hands on the steering wheel

C   Change quickly down the gears

D   Make sure there is nothing behind you

Question 44

What is the legal minimum depth of tread for car tyres?

A   1.6 mm

B   2.5 mm

C   4 mm

D   1 mm

Answers

Question 42

C - When you take your foot off the accelerator, engines have a natural resistance to turn, caused mainly by the cylinder compression. Changing to a lower gear requires the engine to turn faster and so it will have greater resistance than when it's made to turn more slowly. When going downhill, changing to a lower gear will therefore help to keep the vehicle's speed in check.

Question 43

B - If you have to stop in an emergency, you must teach your pupil to react as soon as they can while keeping control of the vehicle. Both hands must be kept on the steering wheel so that they can control the vehicle's direction of travel.

Question 44

A - Car tyres must have sufficient depth of tread to give them a good grip on the road surface. The legal minimum for cars is 1.6 mm. This depth should be across the central three-quarters of the breadth of the tyre and around the entire circumference.

Question 45 *

MOT tests include an exhaust emission test. Why is this carried out?

A To help protect the environment

B To measure your fuel consumption

C To check the engine's power output

D To check which fuel you are using

Question 46 *

What does it mean when the amber light flashes after you have stopped at a pelican crossing?

A You must wait for pedestrians to clear the crossing

B You now have right of way over the pedestrians

C You must still wait for people to step out

D You must wait for the green light before moving off

Question 47

What is a Statutory Off-Road Notification (SORN)?

A A notification to tell DVSA that a vehicle doesn't have a current MOT

B Information held by insurance companies to check a vehicle is insured

C A notification to tell DVLA that a vehicle isn't being used on the road

D Information kept by the police about the owner of a vehicle

Answers

Question 45

A - Emission tests are carried out to make sure your vehicle's engine is operating efficiently. This ensures the pollution produced by the engine is kept to a minimum. If your vehicle isn't serviced regularly, it may fail the annual MOT test.

Question 46

A - Any pedestrians still on the road must be allowed to finish crossing, but anyone on the footpath should not now begin to cross. You may drive on as soon as it is safe to do so.

Question 47

C - A SORN (Statutory Off Road Notification) is used to tell the DVLA that a vehicle in temporarily not in use and it does not require road tax. It must be kept off the road during this time.

Question 48 *

What rules apply to a car that is being used for a driving test?

A   It can be fitted with dual controls, including a dual accelerator that's operable

B   It can be fitted with a dual brake and dual clutch

C   It cannot be fitted with dual controls; they must be removed for the driving test.

D   It must be fitted with a dual brake, clutch and accelerator

Question 49

You are driving in traffic at the speed limit for the road. What should you do if the driver behind is trying to overtake?

A   Move closer to the car ahead, so the driver behind has no room to overtake you

B   Wave the driver behind to overtake when it's safe

C   Keep a steady course and allow the driver behind to overtake

D   Accelerate to move further away from the other driver

Question 50 *

When does the law state that you MUST stop your vehicle?

A   When you have been involved in an accident

B   Before turning right at a major crossroads

C   When a member of the public waves you down

D   When you get an amber warning light on your dashboard

Answers

Question 48

B - Dual controls can be fitted to a driving school or private car for use on a driving test; they are not a requirement however. A dual control accelerator that is operational must not be fitted.

Question 49

C - Keep a steady course to give the driver behind an opportunity to overtake safely. If necessary, slow down. Reacting incorrectly to another driver's impatience can lead to danger.

Question 50

A - The law requires you to stop if you have been involved in an accident. You must exchange details with anyone else involved before continuing.

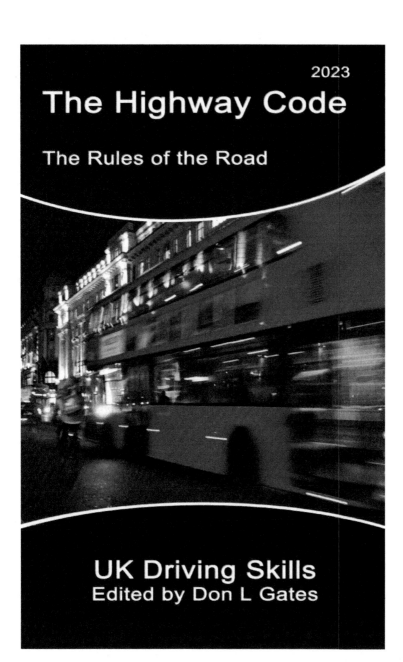

2023
The Highway Code

The Rules of the Road

UK Driving Skills
Edited by Don L Gates

Test Two

Question 1

You are coming up to a roundabout. A cyclist on your left is signalling to turn right. What should you do?

A   Overtake wide on the right

B   Give a warning with your horn

C   Signal the cyclist to move across

D   Stay behind the cyclist

Question 2

What's the main benefit of driving a four-wheel-drive vehicle?

A   Improved grip on the road

B   Lower fuel consumption

C   Shorter stopping distances

D   Improved passenger comfort

Question 3 *

What type of road has direction signs with a green background?

A   Cycle route

B   Tourist route

C   Primary route

D   Urban motorway

Answers

Question 1

D - If you're following a cyclist who's signalling to turn right at a roundabout, stay behind and leave plenty of room.

Although it may not be considered safe by many, the Highway Code states that cyclists may turn right using the left-hand lane; you need to be aware that the rider may cross your path as you approach your exit.

Question 2

A - By driving all four wheels, the vehicle has maximum grip on the road. This grip is especially helpful when travelling on slippery or uneven surfaces. However, having four-wheel drive doesn't replace the skills you need to drive safely.

Question 3

C - Direction signs are colour coded to designate the type of road you are on. Primary routes or 'A' roads have a green background.

Question 4

You're in a tunnel and you see this sign. What does it mean?

A   Beware of pedestrians, no footpath ahead

B   Direction to emergency pedestrian exit

C   No access for pedestrians

D   Beware of pedestrians crossing ahead

Question 5

Why is coasting a bad driving technique?

A   It causes the engine to stall

B   It increases fuel consumption

C   It stops engine braking from slowing the car

D   It makes the engine run faster

Answers

Question 4

B - If you have to leave your vehicle and get out of a tunnel by an emergency exit, do so as quickly as you can. Follow the signs directing you to the nearest exit point.

Question 5

C - When coasting, the engine is disconnected from the drive to the wheels. This means that the engine's resistance can't be used to help slow the vehicle, especially when travelling downhill where the vehicle may actually start to pick up speed.

Question 6

When are anti-lock brakes (ABS) most effective?

A   When you keep pumping the foot brake to prevent skidding

B   When you brake normally but grip the steering wheel tightly

C   When you brake promptly and firmly until you have stopped

D   When you apply the handbrake to reduce the stopping distance

Question 7

You are driving along this road. The driver on the left is reversing from a driveway. What should you do?

A   Move to the opposite side of the road

B   Drive through as you have priority

C   Speed up and drive through quickly

D   Sound your horn and be prepared to stop

Answers

Question 6

C - If you have ABS and need to stop in an emergency, keep your foot firmly on the brake pedal until the vehicle has stopped. When the ABS operates, you may hear a grating sound and feel vibration through the brake pedal. This is normal and you should maintain pressure on the brake pedal until the vehicle stops.

Question 7

D - White lights at the rear of a car show that the driver has selected reverse gear. Sound your horn to warn the other driver of your presence, and reduce your speed as a precaution.

Question 8

Traffic signs giving orders are generally which shape?

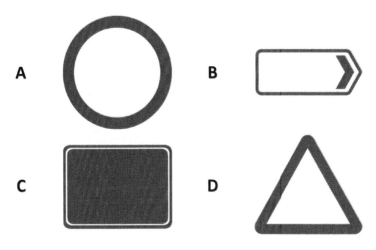

A

B

C

D

Question 9

What is the maximum fine for driving without insurance?

A   £500

B   £1000

C   £5000

D   Unlimited

Answers

Question 8

A - Road signs in the shape of a circle give orders. Those with a red circle are mostly prohibitive. Signs giving orders must always be obeyed.

Question 9

D - Driving without insurance is a serious offence. As well as an unlimited fine, you may be disqualified or incur penalty points

Question 10

Who can accompany a candidate on their driving test?

A   Only their driving instructor

B   Anyone aged 16 or over

C   Only a family member

D   No-one else is allowed in the car

Question 11

There's been a collision. A motorcyclist is lying injured and unconscious. Unless it's essential, why should you not usually attempt to remove their helmet?

A   This could result in more serious injury

B   They might not want you to

C   They'll get too cold if you do this

D   You could scratch the helmet

Question 12

During a driving lesson, your vehicle is involved in a collision. What should you do if your pupil is physically unhurt but is suffering from shock?

A   Encourage them to continue with the lesson to regain confidence

B   Give them reassurance while you wait for help to arrive

C   Suggest that they go home by public transport

D   Tell them that they shouldn't drive for a few weeks

Answers

Question 10

B - At the start of the practical driving test, the examiner will ask the candidate if they wish their instructor or accompanying driver to be present during the test. Anyone who does accompany the candidate must be 16 years or older and must wear a seat belt during the test.

Question 11

A - When someone is injured, any movement that isn't absolutely necessary should be avoided, since it could make the injuries worse. Unless it's essential to remove a motorcyclist's helmet, it's generally safer to leave it in place.

Question 12

B - People who appear uninjured may be in shock and need professional treatment. Avoid unnecessary movement, reassure them, and keep them comfortable and warm. Don't leave them on their own and don't give them anything to eat or drink. Make sure the emergency services are called if necessary.

Question 13

Your pupil is at the end of their driving test. What does DVSA advise you to do?

A   Request a separate debrief

B   Keep out of sight to avoid distraction

C   Request a personal written report

D   Listen to the debrief

Question 14

You think the driver of the vehicle in front has forgotten to cancel their right indicator. What should you do?

A   Flash your lights to alert the driver

B   Turn your right indicator on and off

C   Overtake on the left if there is room

D   Stay behind and don't overtake

Question 15

You are carrying an 11-year-old child in the back seat of your car. They are under 1.35 metres (4 feet 5 inches) tall. What must you make sure of?

A   That they sit between two belted people

B   That they can fasten their own seat belt

C   That a suitable child restraint is available

D   That they can see clearly out of the front window

Answers

Question 13

D - Subject to the candidate's permission, instructors are encouraged to accompany their pupils on their driving test and also to listen to the examiner's debrief. If they haven't been present during the test, instructors are advised to be available to listen to the examiner's debrief at the end of the test.

Question 14

D - Be cautious and don't attempt to overtake. The driver may be unsure of the location of a junction and may turn suddenly. Flashing your lights or using your own indicator is a signal that could easily be misinterpreted by anyone who sees it.

Question 15

C - As the driver, it's your responsibility to make sure that children are secure and safe in your vehicle. Make yourself familiar with the rules. In a few very exceptional cases when a child restraint isn't available, an adult seat belt must be used.

Question 16

At an incident, someone is suffering from severe burns. What should you do to help them?

A   Apply moisturiser to the injuries

B   Wrap the burns in bandages

C   Remove anything sticking to the burns

D   Douse the burns with cool water

Question 17 *

You are teaching someone how to reverse into a side road. When would the greatest hazard to passing traffic occur?

A   After you have entered the side road

B   When the front of your vehicle swings out

C   After you have completed the manoeuvre

D   When you first begin to reverse

Question 18

What it the minimum age to drive a car by a person receiving the higher rate of disability living allowance?

A   15

B   16

C   17

D   18

Answers

Question 16

D - Your priority is to cool the burns with clean, cool water. Its coolness will help take the heat out of the burns and relieve the pain. If possible, keep the wound doused for at least 10 minutes.

Question 17

B - When the front of the vehicle begins to swing out this could endanger oncoming traffic which may not realise that you are reversing. When teaching someone to reverse, make sure that they are aware of this and always teach them to check to the front and side before they begin to steer.

Question 18

B - A 16-year-old person may be issued with a driving licence if they are in receipt of the higher rate of disability living allowance.

Question 19 *

Why would you change into a lower gear after passing this sign?

A   To control your speed using engine braking

B   To provide extra acceleration

C   To give better fuel economy

D   To get more power for the climb

Question 20 *

You are about to move away from the kerb, there is a cyclist fairly close behind you. What should you tell your pupil to do?

A   Signal to let them know you will move off after they have passed

B   Accelerate quickly away before they get to you

C   Signal and start to move slowly forward to give the rider chance to slow down

D   Wait until they have passed before signalling to move off

Answers

Question 19

A - This sign gives you an early warning that the road ahead will slope downhill. Prepare to alter your speed and gear. Looking at the sign from left to right will show you whether the road slopes uphill or downhill.

Question 20

D - Cyclists can feel very vulnerable if the driver of a vehicle signals to move off as they are approaching it. They do not know for sure whether you have seen them and they may think you are about to move. No movement should be made which could intimidate or surprise them. Teach your pupil to show consideration and allow the rider to pass before you even think about signalling.

Question 21 *

You see these markings on the kerbside. When are you allowed to stop there to unload your vehicle?

A   Not at any time

B   During the working day

C   Outside the working day

D   During the times shown

Question 22

How would you identify a section of road used by trams?

A   There would be a different surface texture

B   There would be metal studs around it

C   There would be zigzag markings alongside it

D   There would be yellow hatch markings around it

Answers

Question 21

A - Loading or unloading is not permitted at any time where double yellow stripes mark the kerb edge. A single yellow stripe would allow loading and unloading during times shown on nearby signs.

Question 22

A - Trams may run on roads used by other vehicles and pedestrians. The section of road used by trams is known as the reserved area and should be kept clear. It usually has a different surface, edged with white lane markings.

Question 23

What does this traffic sign mean?

A Hump bridge

B Humps in the road

C Steep camber

D Soft verges

Question 24 *

You are waiting in a traffic queue at night. What should you do to avoid dazzling other drivers?

A Apply the parking brake only

B Apply the footbrake only

C Switch off your headlights

D Use both the parking brake and footbrake

Answers

Question 23

B - These humps have been put in place to slow the traffic down. They're usually found in residential areas. Slow down to an appropriate speed.

Question 24

A - Brake lights are bright and can dazzle anyone waiting behind you if you keep your foot on the brake pedal. Applying the parking brake instead will prevent this.

Question 25

You are looking for somewhere to park your vehicle. The area is full except for spaces marked 'disabled use'. What can you do?

A   You can use these spaces when elsewhere is full

B   You can park in one of these spaces if you stay with your vehicle

C   You can use one of the spaces as long as one is kept free

D   You can't park there, unless you are permitted to do so

Question 26 *

What does this red cross on a blue background mean?

A   No waiting

B   No stopping

C   No entry

D   No vehicles

Answers

Question 25

D - It's illegal to park in a space reserved for disabled users unless you're permitted to do so. These spaces are provided for people with limited mobility, who may need extra space to get in and out of their vehicle.

Question 26

B - The sign indicates that the road is a 'clearway' where no stopping is allowed. There may also be an information plate telling you what times this restriction is in force. If there is no time plate, you should assume that the clearway is in operation 24 hours.

Question 27

You are teaching a pupil to move off from the side of the road. Why should you teach them to look around?

A   Because the mirrors may not be adjusted properly

B   To avoid failing their driving test

C   To check for road signs and speed limits

D   To check that there is nothing in the blind spot

Question 28 *

What does this arrow marking in the middle of the road mean?

A   Traffic should use the hard shoulder

B   The road is about to bend to the left

C   Overtaking drivers should move back to the left

D   It is a safe place to overtake

Answers

Question 27

D - There are always blind spots that mirrors don't cover. It's important that instructors explain that safety checks aren't just a test requirement but are a vital part of keeping safe on the road. Explaining the reasons behind safety checks should help pupils to think for themselves and become safer drivers.

Question 28

C - The white arrow warns any overtaking drivers that they should move back to the left. There is probably a hazard ahead such as a dip in the road, a bend, or a traffic island.

Question 29

After passing the driving test. What's the maximum authorised mass (MAM) of any trailer that can be towed?

A   2,500 kg

B   4,500 kg

C   3,500 kg

D   5,500 kg

Question 30

You give instruction in short, progressive steps. What is this teaching technique likely to lead to?

A   A sense of boredom in the pupil

B   Sustained interest from the pupil

C   The completion of the lesson in a shorter time

D   A lack of coordination in driving the vehicle

Question 31

What colour are the reflective studs between a motorway and its slip road?

A   Amber

B   White

C   Green

D   Red

Answers

Question 29

C - When you pass your driving test, you're allowed to tow a trailer up to 3,500 kg MAM without taking an extra test.

If you want to tow a heavier trailer, you'll have to pass either a CE or DE category test, dependent on the towing vehicle.

Question 30

B - An interested pupil is likely to be well motivated and should retain information better than one who has lost interest. Everyone has different abilities, so instruction needs to be varied to suit the individual.

Question 31

C - The studs between the carriageway and the hard shoulder are normally red. These change to green where there's a slip road, helping you to identify slip roads when visibility is poor or when it's dark.

Question 32

Your car requires an MOT certificate. When is it legal to drive it without an MOT certificate?

A   Up to seven days after the old certificate has run out

B   When driving to an appointment at an MOT centre

C   When driving to an MOT centre to arrange an appointment

D   When driving the car with the owner's permission

Question 33

You are following a slower-moving vehicle. There is a junction just ahead on the right. What should you do?

A   Overtake after checking your mirrors and signalling

B   Only consider overtaking when you are past the junction

C   Accelerate quickly to pass before the junction

D   Slow down and prepare to overtake on the left

Answers

Question 32

B - When a car is three years old (four years old in Northern Ireland), it must pass an MOT test and have a valid MOT certificate before it can be used on the road. Exceptionally, you may

- drive to a pre-arranged test appointment or to a garage for repairs required for the test
- drive vehicles made before 1960 without an MOT test, but they must be in a roadworthy condition before being used on the road.

Question 33

B - You should never overtake as you approach a junction. If a vehicle emerged from the junction while you were overtaking, a dangerous situation could develop very quickly.

Question 34

At a junction, you see this sign partly covered by snow. What does it mean?

A   Crossroads

B   Give way

C   Stop

D   No entry

Question 35

You are the first to arrive at the scene of a serious incident. What should you do?

A   Leave as soon as another motorist arrives

B   Flag down other motorists to help you

C   Drag all casualties away from the vehicles

D   Call the emergency services promptly

Answers

Question 34

C - The 'stop' sign is the only road sign that's octagonal. This is so that it can be recognised and obeyed even if it's obscured (for example, by snow).

Question 35

D - At a crash scene you can help in practical ways, even if you aren't trained in first aid. Call the emergency services and make sure you don't put yourself or anyone else in danger. The safest way to warn other traffic is by switching on your hazard warning lights.

Question 36

What should you do if your anti-lock brake (ABS) warning light stays on?

A   Check the brake-fluid level

B   Check the footbrake free play

C   Make sure this is corrected at your next service

D   Have the brakes checked as soon as possible

Question 37

What do these signs count down to?

A   A primary road junction

B   A roadside rest area

C   A service station

D   A concealed level crossing

Answers

Question 36

D - Consult the vehicle handbook or a garage before driving the vehicle any further. Only drive to a garage if it's safe to do so. If you aren't sure, get expert help.

Question 37

D - You will find these were there is a level crossing which is hidden from view. When you see these signs, reduce your speed. You may well have to stop at the level crossing, or there may already be traffic queuing ahead.

Question 38 *

You've been following a slow-moving motorcyclist for quite a while.
What should you do if you're unsure what the rider is going to do?

A   Go quickly past on their left

B   Go quickly past on their right

C   Tap the horn before carefully overtaking

D   Stay behind them and keep your distance

Question 39

You are driving towards this left-hand bend. What should you tell your
pupil to be most aware of?

A   A change in speed limit

B   The lack of road markings

C   The lack of a sign to warn you of the bend

D   Pedestrians walking towards you

Answers

Question 38

C - Initially you should stay behind and keep your distance, but there may come a point when they are causing a problem for you and following traffic. You need to make them aware of your presence with a light tap on the horn. If they continue to ride at very low speed then you may then cautiously overtake if it's safe.

Question 39

D - Pedestrians walking on a road with no pavement should walk against the direction of the traffic. You can't see around this bend: there may be hidden dangers. Always keep this in mind and give yourself time to react if a hazard does appear.

Question 40

What is the routine for preparing to move off downhill?

A   Engage a high gear; ride the clutch until the correct speed has been reached

B   Engage first gear; press the accelerator slightly; release the parking brake

C   Engage the appropriate gear; release the footbrake and parking brake together

D   Engage the appropriate gear; apply the footbrake; release the parking brake, keeping the footbrake applied

Question 41

What does the law require you to keep in good condition?

A   Seat belt

B   Gears

C   Transmission

D   Door locks

Answers

Question 40

D - When a vehicle is facing downhill, it will try to roll forward when the parking brake is released. Applying the footbrake before releasing the parking brake ensures control is maintained.

Question 41

A - Unless exempt, you and your passengers must wear a seat belt (or suitable child restraint). The seat belts in your car must be in good condition and working properly; they'll be checked during its MOT test.

Question 42

What does this sign mean?

A End of two-way road

B Give priority to vehicles coming towards you

C You have priority over vehicles coming towards you

D Start of two-way road

Question 43 *

You want your pupil to reverse park a car between two vehicles on the side of the road. As a guide, what would be the minimum size for a suitable parking space?

A Three car lengths

B Two car lengths

C Two and a half car lengths

D One and a half car lengths

Answers

Question 42

C - You may have priority but don't force your way through. Show courtesy and consideration to other road users. Even though you have priority, make sure oncoming traffic is going to give way before you continue.

Question 43

D - Reverse or parallel parking between parked vehicles is an essential skill to master. How large the space needs to be depends on the driver's skill and the size of their car. A basic guideline would be a minimum space of one and a half times the length of their car.

Question 44 *

Your pupil has just failed their driving test. What will the examiner give them?

A   Advice on how to be better prepared for the next time

B   An application form for another driving test

C   Advice about how many more hours of training they need

D   An explanation of any serious or dangerous faults committed during the test

Question 45

You are driving on an open road in dry weather. What should the minimum distance be between you and the vehicle in front?

A   A two-second time gap

B   One car length

C   A two metre gap (6 feet 6 inches)

D   Two car lengths

Question 46 *

You see a pedestrian approaching a zebra crossing. What should you expect your pupil to do?

A   Accelerate before they step onto the crossing

B   Stop and wave at them to cross the road

C   Slow down and allow them to cross if they want to

D   Ignore them as they are still on the pavement

Answers

Question 44

D - The examiner will give a brief explanation of the faults committed during the test to help the candidate understand why they were not successful. A copy of the faults marked will be sent to the email address they have provided.

Question 45

A - One way of checking there's a safe distance between you and the vehicle in front is to use the two-second rule. To check for a two-second time gap, choose a stationary object ahead, such as a bridge or road sign. When the car in front passes the object, say 'Only a fool breaks the two-second rule'. If you reach the object before you finish saying the phrase, you're too close and need to increase the gap.

Question 46

C - Pedestrians have right of way once they step onto the crossing, but you should always instruct your pupils to slow down and be ready to stop to allow them to step out. Never allow them to take control of someone else's safety by waving them onto the road; they may step into some other danger.

Question 47

Is it necessary to give a signal when you're passing parked vehicles?

A It's only necessary when there's traffic behind

B It's only necessary when there's oncoming traffic

C It might not be necessary

D It's always necessary

Question 48

You are approaching a red light at a puffin crossing. Pedestrians are on the crossing. When will the red light change?

A When you start to edge forward onto the crossing

B When the pedestrians have cleared the crossing

C When the pedestrians push the button on the other side

D When a driver from the opposite direction reaches the crossing

Question 49

Why should you test your brakes after driving through a ford?

A To check your brake lights are working

B To make sure you can stop safely

C To bleed air from the brake system

D To remove the water from your tyres

Answers

Question 47

C - A signal might not be necessary where there's no-one to benefit from it, or where the signal could confuse other road users. Forward planning and taking an early and steady course will remove the need to routinely signal to pass parked vehicles or obstructions.

Question 48

B - A sensor will automatically detect that the pedestrians have reached a safe position. Don't drive on until the green light shows and it's safe for you to do so.

Question 49

B - At a ford, the road passes through a stream at a place where the water is normally shallow. When you've gone through the water, you should test your brakes and if necessary dry them out. To do this, first check that you won't cause danger to traffic behind. Then apply a light brake pressure while moving slowly. Make sure your brakes are working properly before resuming normal driving.

Question 50 *

What should you tell your pupil to do when you see an emergency vehicle behind you?

A   Move aside and slow down when it is safe

B   Continue normally and let them decide when to pass

C   Maintain your speed but signal left to let them know they can pass

D   Brake to an immediate stop until they pass

Answers

Question 50

A - You should do what you can to let the emergency vehicle pass, but do not suddenly stop as this could take others by surprise and cause danger in itself. Reduce speed and move over to the left as soon as it is safe to do so.

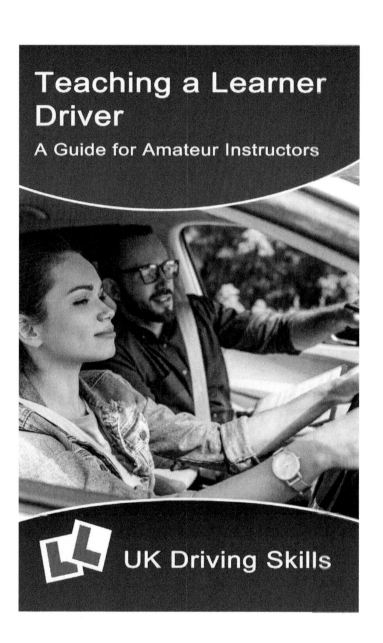

Teaching a Learner Driver
A Guide for Amateur Instructors

UK Driving Skills

Test Three

Question 1

Which sign means 'uneven road'?

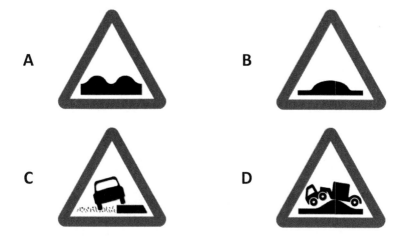

A

B

C

D

Question 2

A casualty isn't breathing normally and needs CPR. At what rate should you press down and release on the centre of their chest?

A   10 per minute

B   120 per minute

C   60 per minute

D   240 per minute

Answers

Question 1

A - Some signs can look similar to others but each one has a different meaning. Ensure that you are familiar with all the traffic signs so that you can pass on this knowledge to your pupils.

Question 2

B - If a casualty isn't breathing normally, cardiopulmonary resuscitation (CPR) may be needed to maintain circulation. Place two hands on the centre of the chest and press down hard and fast, around 5 - 6 centimetres and about twice a second.

Question 3

You are travelling along a motorway. When are you allowed to overtake on the left?

A   If you're within one mile of your exit

B   If the driver ahead won't move over to let you pass

C   If you're in stationary traffic but the hard shoulder is clear

D   If you're driving in a slow-moving traffic queue

Question 4 *

After servicing your own car, what should you do with the old oil?

A   Take it to an official disposal and recycling site

B   Mix it with some detergent before pouring it into the drain

C   Pour it into the soil and top with sand

D   Put it into a bottle and place in your recycle bin

Question 5

What should you do if you park on the road when it's foggy?

A   Leave dipped headlights and fog lights switched on

B   Leave dipped headlights switched on

C   Leave sidelights switched on

D   Leave main-beam headlights switched on

Answers

Question 3

D - Never overtake on the left, unless the traffic is moving in queues and the queue on your right is moving more slowly than the one you're in. Don't be tempted to keep changing lanes to join a faster queue; you'll find they all slow down and speed up at various intervals.

Question 4

A - Engine oil is full of toxins and pollutants which should only be disposed of safely by taking it to an official recycling site.

Question 5

C - If you have to park your vehicle in foggy conditions, try to find a place to park off the road. If this isn't possible, park on the road facing in the same direction as the traffic. Leave your sidelights switched on and make sure they're clean.

Question 6

What does this sign mean?

A   Queues likely

B   Car lane only

C   Single file traffic

D   Keep your distance

Question 7 *

Your pupil is waiting to turn right into a side road. An oncoming driver slows down and flashes their lights. What should you tell your pupil to do?

A   To make the turn as quickly as possible

B   To ignore the other driver and stay where they are

C   To make the turn after checking that it's safe to do so

D   To stay where they are and wave the other driver on

Answers

Question 6

A - When you see this sign, beware of traffic queues ahead. Check your mirrors and reduce your speed.

Be patient when you're delayed by traffic queues and reduce the possibility of being involved in an incident. Research shows that you make poor decisions when you're angry, so you're less likely to spot and respond safely to hazards.

Question 7

C - The flashing of headlights has the same meaning as sounding the horn: it's a warning of someone's presence. We all know however that many drivers misuse it as a signal for another driver to go ahead. Before turning your pupil needs to be aware of certain things:

- That the signal is meant for them
- That the other driver is definitely waiting
- That there are no pedestrians crossing the side road
- That no other vehicles are about to pass the other driver, particularly cyclists and motorcyclists who may be hidden from view.

Question 8

What restrictions are placed on someone's driving licence if they are blind in one eye?

A   They are not permitted to drive a motor car

B   They are only permitted to drive while they are wearing glasses

C   Their driving licence is not restricted in any way

D   They are required to have additional mirrors fitted to any car they drive

Question 9 *

Which of the following would make your tyres illegal?

A   Having a deep cut in the sidewall

B   Having tyres of different tread patterns

C   Having different makes of tyre on the same axle

D   Having less than 1.6 mm of tread on the outer edge

Question 10

You're on a motorway. Red flashing lights appear above your lane only. What should you do?

A   Continue in that lane and look for further information

B   Move into another lane in good time

C   Pull onto the hard shoulder

D   Stop and wait for an instruction to proceed

Answers

Question 8

C - A person with only one eye isn't considered to have a disability for the purpose of driving and will be issued with an unrestricted driving licence.

Question 9

A - Your tyres may be of different treads and makes as long as they're in good condition. They must, however, be intact, without cuts or tears. When checking the side walls for cuts and bulges, don't forget to check the side of the tyre that's hidden from view, under the car.

Question 10

B - Flashing red lights above your lane show that your lane is closed. You should move into another lane as soon as it's safe to do so.

Question 11

A pupil who normally wears glasses when driving wants to wear sunglasses on the day of their driving test. What should you do?

A   Tell them that they can be used for the eyesight check but not for driving

B   Say nothing, it's up to them what kind of eyewear they choose to use.

C   Tell them that they are not allowed to wear sunglasses during the test.

D   Ask if the sunglasses have the same prescription as their normal glasses.

Question 12

You break down on a motorway. You need to call for help. Why may it be better to use an emergency roadside telephone rather than a mobile phone?

A   It connects you to a local garage

B   Using a mobile phone will distract other drivers

C   It allows easy location by the emergency services

D   Mobile phones don't work on motorways

Answers

Question 11

D - It is perfectly acceptable to wear sunglasses during lessons and during the driving test. However, if the pupil normally needs to wear glasses then these must also be prescription glasses matching the specification of their normal lenses. You should always ask to make sure of this before you allow them to wear them while driving.

Question 12

C - On a motorway, it's best to use a roadside emergency telephone so that the emergency services are able to find you easily. The location of the nearest telephone is shown by an arrow on marker posts at the edge of the hard shoulder. If you use a mobile, the operator will need to know your exact location. Before you call, find out the number on the nearest marker post. This number will identify your exact location.

Question 13 *

Why should you slow down when you see this sign?

A   There is broken glass from an accident

B   There is standing water on the road

C   There is a risk of falling rocks

D   There are loose chippings on the road

Question 14 *

What does this sign mean?

A   Dual-carriageway ends

B   Merging traffic on both sides

C   There is a fork in the road

D   Road narrows both sides

Answers

Question 13

D - When a road has been resurfaced with loose chippings there is a risk that these can shoot out from under vehicle tyres. The danger is that the chippings can then damage paintwork, crack windscreens, and even injure cyclists and motorcyclists. There will be an advisory speed limit which you should obey until the chippings are well bedded down.

Question 14

D - The road is about to narrow on both sides, you need to be more aware of any overtaking or oncoming traffic.

Question 15 *

Following a long spell of hot dry weather, it's now starting to rain. What do you need to be aware of?

A   There may be an increased risk of skidding

B   The cleaner road surface will give a better grip

C   Braking distances will be shortened

D   The road surface may start to break up

Question 16

You've just passed these flashing warning lights at the side of the road. What hazard would you expect to see next?

A   A school crossing patrol

B   A level crossing with no barrier

C   An ambulance station

D   An opening bridge

Answers

Question 15

A - Oil and rubber can build up on the road during long spells of dry weather. When it rains, this can make the road surface very slippery. You should make allowances for this when braking and cornering.

Question 16

A - Activated by a school crossing patrol, these lights warn that children may be crossing the road to a nearby school. Slow down so that you're ready to stop if necessary.

Question 17

Which drivers are given instructions by diamond-shaped signs?

A   Drivers of lorries

B   Drivers of buses

C   Drivers of trams

D   Drivers of tractors

Question 18

What should you do if a pupil you are instructing fails to make the progress you were expecting?

A   Be patient and continue the well-tried methods that are working with other pupils

B   Ask the pupil if there is a particular problem that is holding them back

C   Go on to more advanced driving situations to speed up the learning process

D   Continue to repeat the same exercise until the pupil gets it right

Answers

Question 17

C - You need to show caution when driving in areas where trams operate. There may also be crossing points where you'll need to give way to them, or areas specifically reserved for trams, which you aren't allowed to enter.

Question 18

B - If your usual techniques or methods don't appear to be working, you should discuss the matter with your pupil, and explore alternative ways of getting the point across.

Question 19

You arrive at an incident. There is no danger from fire or further collisions. What is your first priority when attending to an unconscious motorcyclist?

A Check whether they are breathing normally

B Check whether they are bleeding

C Check whether they have any broken bones

D Check whether their helmet can be removed

Question 20 *

How is overtaking in a one-way street different from overtaking on a two-way road?

A Overtaking is not allowed

B You can only overtake on the left-hand side

C You can only overtake on the right-hand side

D You can overtake on either side

Question 21

You are about to emerge from a junction. Your passenger tells you it is clear. When should you rely on their judgement?

A Never; you should always look for yourself

B When the roads are very busy

C When the roads are very quiet

D Only when they are a qualified driver

Answers

Question 19

A - At the scene of an incident, always be aware of danger from further collisions or fire. The first priority when dealing with an unconscious person is to ensure they're breathing normally. If they're having difficulty breathing, follow the DR ABC code.

Question 20

D - In a one-way street you can overtake on the left or the right. You should take up an appropriate lane or position for your destination in good time.

Question 21

A - Your passenger may be inexperienced in judging traffic situations, may have a poor view or may not have seen a potential hazard. You're responsible for your own safety and that of your passenger. Always make your own checks to be sure it's safe to pull out.

Question 22 *

You are driving on a single track road which is only wide enough for one vehicle. What should you do if another car comes towards you?

A   Pull into a passing place on your right

B   Reverse until the road becomes wider

C   Drive onto the grass verge

D   Pull into a passing place on your left

Question 23 *

What does this traffic sign mean?

A   No parking allowed

B   Parking for cars only

C   Only motor cars allowed

D   No motor cars allowed

Answers

Question 22

D - Narrow roads such as this usually have passing places where the road is widened to make room for two vehicles to pass. You should plan well ahead and be prepared to pull into a space on your left. If there is a closer space on your right, you should stop and wait opposite or just before it. Driving onto the grass verge should be avoided wherever possible, as there may be hidden dips or soft earth where you may become stuck.

Question 23

D - Drivers of motor cars are not allowed to proceed beyond this sign.

Question 24

What should you do if you're signalled to stop by a police officer in a patrol car?

A   Stop on the left as soon as it's safe

B   Wait until they turn on the blue light before stopping

C   Carry on until you reach a side road

D   Stop immediately wherever you are

Question 25 *

What should you do before making a journey when it is snowing?

A   Ask yourself whether you really need to travel

B   Avoid carrying too many passengers

C   Plan a route avoiding open roads

D   Make sure that your air conditioning is working

Question 26

When can you park on the verge or footpath?

A   When parking signs allow it

B   To load and unload

C   When you're stopping outside retail premises

D   To pick up passengers

Answers

Question 24

A - If a police officer signals for you to stop, keep calm, think before you act, and stop as soon as possible in a safe place on the left.

Question 25

A - Driving in snow should always be avoided wherever possible. There is always a greater risk of accidents and breakdowns when the weather is bad. You need to ask yourself if you really do need to travel.

Question 26

A - Generally, vehicles shouldn't park partially or fully on verges, footpaths or pavements. However, it's becoming more common for this to be allowed on some narrow streets. Special parking signs will show where it's allowed.

Question 27

On a motorway, what is an emergency refuge area used for?

A   For when your vehicle has broken down

B   If you think you'll be involved in a road rage incident

C   For a police patrol to park and watch traffic

D   For construction and road workers to store emergency equipment

Question 28 *

You are driving on the left of this road. When may you cross the centre lines?

A   You must not cross them at all

B   When overtaking another driver

C   When passing an obstruction

D   When you can see it is clear ahead

Answers

Question 27

A - Emergency refuge areas are built at the side of the hard shoulder. If you break down, try to get your vehicle into the refuge, where there's an emergency telephone. The phone connects directly to a control centre. Remember to take care when rejoining the motorway, especially if the hard shoulder is being used as a running lane.

Question 28

C - With double white lines, if the nearest line to you is solid then you may only cross it in certain circumstances. One of those is if you have to pass a stationary obstruction.

Question 29 *

You see a learner driver starting to pull out of a junction close on your left. What action should you take?

A   Reduce speed and be ready to pull back in case they continue

B   Carry on as normal as their instructor will stop them

C   Slow down and wave them out of the junction

D   Move into a wide position so that you can pass them if they pull out

Question 30 *

You are on a busy dual-carriageway; the following driver is much too close to your rear. What can you do to lower the risk?

A   Increase the gap between you and the vehicle ahead

B   Pick up speed to increase the distance behind

C   Slow right down until the other driver overtakes

D   Signal left to let the other driver know they can overtake

Question 31

You're at a junction controlled by traffic lights. When shouldn't you proceed at green?

A   When pedestrians are waiting to cross

B   When you intend to turn right

C   When you think the lights may be about to change

D   When your exit from the junction is blocked

Answers

Question 29

A - Learner drivers can be unpredictable and may lose control of the car. You should be courteous and maintain a safe distance, allowing for any mistakes that they might make. Never wave other road users on; you may put them into danger from someone else.

Question 30

A - If they wish to overtake at any point, you should leave that decision up to them and maintain a steady speed while gradually opening up space ahead. If you have plenty of space in front, then you will have more time to react if traffic suddenly slows down. This will lessen the risk of the following driver running into you.

Question 31

D - As you approach the lights, look into the road you wish to take. Only proceed if your exit road is clear. If the road is blocked, hold back, even if you have to wait for the next green signal.

Question 32

You are convicted of driving after drinking too much alcohol. How could this affect your insurance?

A Your insurance may become invalid

B The amount of excess you pay will be reduced

C You will only be able to get third-party cover

D Cover will only be given for driving smaller cars

Question 33 *

When are you allowed to drive along this bus lane with your pupil?

A Not at any time

B Only on a weekend

C During the times shown

D Outside of the times shown

Answers

Question 32

A - Driving while under the influence of drink or drugs can invalidate your insurance. It also endangers yourself and others. The risk isn't worth taking.

Question 33

D - This bus lane is only in operation between 7 to 10 a.m. and 4 to 6:30 p.m. from Monday to Friday. Outside of those times any vehicle can use the lane for normal driving.

Question 34

What major advantage does a pupil gain from agreeing learning objectives?

A They will know what is expected of them and be able to evaluate their progress

B They will be able to drive a vehicle responsibly, with concentration and patience

C They will have no need to ask questions of the instructor

D They will know when they are ready to take the test

Question 35 *

What should you do if a trailer starts to swing from side to side while you're towing it?

A Let go of the steering wheel and let it correct itself

B Steer in the direction the trailer is swinging

C Accelerate gradually until it stabilises

D Ease off the accelerator to reduce your speed

Question 36

What's the nearest you may park to a junction?

A 10 metres (32 feet)

B 12 metres (39 feet)

C 15 metres (49 feet)

D 20 metres (66 feet)

Answers

Question 34

A - Agreeing learning should be a two-way process. You can contribute your understanding of what has to be achieved and the learner can contribute their objectives and understanding. At the end of a lesson, both you and the pupil will be better placed to evaluate progress.

Question 35

D - Strong winds or buffeting from large vehicles can cause a trailer or caravan to swing from side to side ('snake'). If this happens, ease off the accelerator. Don't brake, steer sharply or increase your speed.

Question 36

A - Don't park within 10 metres (32 feet) of a junction (unless in an authorised parking place). This is to allow drivers emerging from, or turning into the junction a clear view of the road they're joining. It also allows them to see hazards such as pedestrians or cyclists at the junction.

Question 37 *

What type of vehicle might you see with a flashing green light on top?

A   An agricultural vehicle

B   A road sweeper

C   An invalid carriage

D   An emergency doctor's car

Question 38

You've broken down on a motorway. In which direction should you walk to find the nearest emergency telephone?

A   With the traffic flow

B   In the direction shown on the marker posts

C   Facing oncoming traffic

D   In the direction of the nearest exit

Question 39

What advice should you give to someone who intends to drive a left-hand drive vehicle in the UK?

A   Give signals earlier

B   Keep well to the left of your lane

C   Make full use of the mirrors

D   Use hand signals when turning

Answers

Question 37

D - A doctor is allowed to put a flashing green light on top of their car when they are on an emergency call. If you see one of these you should give way to them if you can do so safely.

Question 38

B - Along the hard shoulder there are marker posts at 100-metre intervals. These will direct you to the nearest emergency telephone.

Question 39

C - In a left-hand-drive vehicle, use of the mirrors and awareness of blind areas is very important. Being seated on the car's left makes the blind area on your right more difficult to overcome. For example, when joining a dual carriageway or motorway from a slip road, traffic on the carriageway will be approaching in the blind area on your right and could easily be overlooked.

Question 40 *

Why do some motorways have variable speed limits?

A   To reduce traffic bunching at peak times

B   To encourage eco-safe driving methods

C   To compensate for poor road surfaces

D   To keep noise down when passing urban areas

Question 41

The road outside this school is marked with yellow zig-zag lines. What do these lines mean?

A   You may park here when dropping off schoolchildren

B   You may park here when picking up schoolchildren

C   You mustn't wait or park your vehicle here at all

D   You must stay with your vehicle if you park here

Answers

Question 40

A - Variable speed limits are used when traffic is busy, and when there are incidents and lane closures. This helps to keep traffic moving at a steady varying speed instead of the 'stop start' situation which normally occurs at these times.

Question 41

C - Parking here would block other road users' view of the school entrance and would endanger the lives of children crossing the road on their way to and from school. The area marked by these lines must be kept clear.

Question 42

What does this sign mean?

A   Side winds

B   Airport ahead

C   Slippery road

D   Flooding

Question 43 *

What does this road sign mean?

A   No parking on the right

B   No cars are allowed

C   Two-way traffic

D   No overtaking

Answers

Question 42

A - You may see this sign in areas where the road is surrounded by open ground. You need to be aware that strong crosswinds could blow you off course.

Question 43

D - You must not overtake any other motor vehicle when you see this sign by the road.

Question 44

Which of the following types of glasses shouldn't be worn when driving at night?

A   Half-moon

B   Varifocal

C   Bifocal

D   Tinted

Question 45

You're parking your car facing uphill with a kerb on your left. You apply the parking brake. What else should you do for added security?

A   Leave the front wheels turned to the left, with the car in first gear

B   Leave the front wheels turned to the left, with the vehicle in reverse gear

C   Leave the front wheels turned to the right, with the vehicle in first gear

D   Leave the front wheels turned to the right, with the vehicle in reverse gear

Answers

Question 44

D - If you're driving at night or in poor visibility, tinted lenses will reduce the efficiency of your vision by reducing the amount of light reaching your eyes.

Question 45

C - Should the parking brake fail, the use of first gear will help to prevent the vehicle from rolling backwards. By turning the front wheels to the right, they'll travel the shortest distance before running against the kerb. This will reduce the potential for the vehicle to move any further.

Question 46 *

Which of the following will have an effect on the stopping distance of your car?

A   The traffic ahead of you

B   The condition of your tyres

C   The light conditions

D   The position of following traffic

Question 47 *

What does this sign mean?

A   No motor vehicles

B   Motor cars and motorcycles only

C   Motorcycles have priority

D   All vehicles prohibited

Answers

Question 46

B - There are a number of factors which will affect the distance it takes for you to stop. One of the most important is the condition of your tyres. You should make a regular check to ensure that they are in good condition and have a good amount of tread on them.

Question 47

A - The sign prohibits all motor vehicles from proceeding. Cyclists, horse drawn carriages etc. are still allowed to continue.

Question 48 *

What does this warning light on the instrument panel mean?

A   Low oil pressure

B   Battery discharge

C   Braking-system fault

D   A door is open

Question 49

You're driving on a motorway. The car in front shows its hazard warning lights for a short time. What does this tell you?

A   There's a police speed check ahead

B   The driver wants you to overtake

C   The other car is going to change lanes

D   Traffic ahead is slowing or stopping suddenly

Answers

Question 48

C - If this warning sign lights up on your dashboard you should call for help and get your brake system checked immediately.

Question 49

D - If the vehicle in front shows its hazard warning lights, there may be an incident or queuing traffic ahead. By keeping a safe distance from the vehicle in front, you're able to look beyond it and see any hazards well ahead.

Question 50 *

You are waiting to turn right out of a minor road. A large vehicle is approaching steadily from your right. You have time to emerge in front of it but why should you tell your pupil to wait?

A   The large vehicle is limiting your view

B   Priority should always be given to large vehicles

C   The other driver may decide to turn

D   A learner driver may stall at the junction

Answers

Question 50

A - A large vehicle will block your view to the right, and there could be an overtaking vehicle which is hidden from view, particularly a motorcyclist. It may be safer to wait until you are certain that nothing is hidden in the blind area.

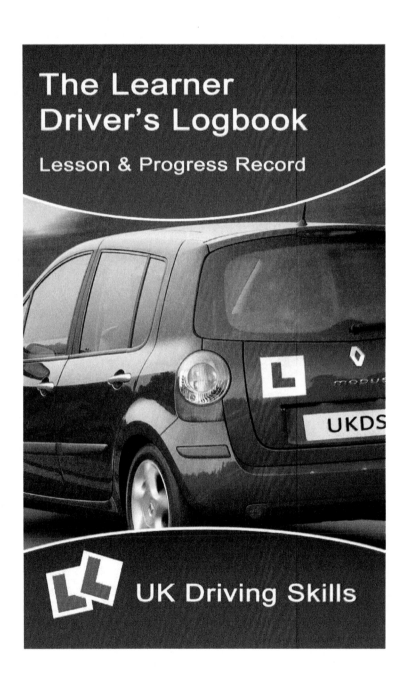

The Learner Driver's Logbook

Lesson & Progress Record

UK Driving Skills

Test Four

Question 1

You're travelling in very heavy rain. How is this likely to affect your overall stopping distance?

A   It will be halved

B   It will be five times longer

C   It will be about the same

D   It will be doubled

Question 2 *

You want to continue ahead at a crossroads where there are no road markings. There are other vehicles approaching from your right and left. Who has priority?

A   No-one has priority

B   The vehicle from the right

C   The vehicle from the left

D   You have priority

Question 3

You're parked in a busy high street. What's the safest way to turn your vehicle around so you can go the opposite way?

A   Drive into a side road and reverse into the main road

B   Get someone to stop the traffic

C   Do a u-turn in the main road

D   Find a side road to turn around in

Answers

Question 1

D - The road will be very wet and spray from other vehicles will reduce your visibility. Tyre grip will also be reduced, increasing your stopping distance. You should at least double your separation distance.

Question 2

A - No-one has priority in this situation. Unmarked crossroads should be approached with plenty of caution. Slow down, take good observation in all directions before you emerge or make a turn. Proceed only when you're sure it's safe to do so.

Question 3

D - Make sure you carry out the manoeuvre without causing a hazard to other vehicles. Choose a place to turn that's safe and convenient for you and for other road users. You should NEVER reverse onto a road from a side street.

Question 4 *

Which of these is likely to be the cause of excessive or uneven tyre wear?

A   Crossing your hands when steering

B   Incorrect use of the gears

C   A fault in the braking system

D   Incorrect operation of the clutch

Question 5 *

What should you do to avoid wheel-spin when driving on ice and snow?

A   By avoiding use of the parking brake

B   By using higher gears than normal

C   By using the ABS braking system

D   By staying in low gears

Question 6 *

When is it acceptable to turn on front fog lights?

A   As soon as mist begins to form

B   As a replacement for main beam headlights

C   When it is starting to get dark

D   When visibility is seriously reduced

Answers

Question 4

C - If you see that parts of the tread on your tyres are wearing before others, it may indicate a brake, steering or suspension fault. Regular servicing will help to detect faults at an early stage and this will avoid the risk of minor faults becoming serious or even dangerous.

Question 5

B - There is less turn of the wheels for any given amount of acceleration when using a higher gear. If you're travelling on an icy road, extra caution will be required to avoid loss of control. Keeping your speed down and using the highest gear possible will reduce the risk of the tyres losing their grip on this slippery surface.

Question 6

D - It is against the law to use fog lights except when visibility is 'seriously reduced'; that is down to less than 100 m (328 feet). If they are used in better conditions they can dazzle other road users. You should make sure when you do have to use them, that you turn them off again as soon as visibility improves.

Question 7 *

After the registration of a new car, when must it first be taken for an MOT inspection?

A   One year

B   Two years

C   Three years

D   Four years

Question 8

What's the most important task at the end of every driving lesson?

A   Set the objectives for the next lesson

B   Arrange the time for the next lesson

C   Go over all the mistakes that have been made

D   Encourage the pupil to reflect on their own performance

Question 9 *

Why should you not leave a roof rack attached to your driving school car during lessons?

A   It will reduce the stopping distance

B   It will use up more fuel than normal

C   It will not be allowed on a school car

D   It will make emergency stops difficult

Answers

Question 7

C - New cars must be taken for their first MOT three years after their first registration, and again every year after that in order to ensure that they are kept in roadworthy condition.

Question 8

D - Giving the pupil a chance to reflect on their own performance helps them to consolidate their learning and to raise any issues that are concerning them. It gives the instructor a clearer insight into what the pupil is thinking and provides a good foundation for agreeing what to do in the next lesson.

Question 9

B - Despite the relatively small size of a roof rack, if it is left on the vehicle unnecessarily it will cause drag and result extra fuel usage. This can add up to a surprising amount of waste over a period of time and it should always be removed when not in use.

Question 10

What does this sign mean?

A   End of cycle route

B   End of clearway

C   End of restricted speed area

D   End of restricted parking area

Question 11

You're carrying a child in your car. They're under three years old. Which of these is a suitable restraint?

A   A child seat

B   An adult lap belt

C   An adult holding a child

D   A normal seat belt

Answers

Question 10

D - Even though you've left the restricted area, make sure that you park where you won't endanger other road users or cause an obstruction.

Question 11

A - Suitable restraints include a child seat, baby seat, booster seat or booster cushion. It's essential that any restraint used is suitable for the child's size and weight, and fitted according to the manufacturer's instructions.

Question 12 *

You're going to be driving a long distance at motorway speeds. Your car is carrying passengers and luggage. What should you do to the tyre pressures?

A   Reduce pressure in all the tyres

B   Increase pressure in the rear tyres

C   Increase pressure in all the tyres

D   Reduce pressure in the rear tyres

Question 13

A pupil with a physical disability is concerned that the examiner will not understand their special needs. What should you tell them?

A   All examiners are trained to assess the driving of candidates with special needs

B   They'll have to be much better than an able-bodied driver

C   The examiner will have more time to study their faults

D   They'll be tested to a lower standard than an able-bodied driver

Question 14

What does a sign with a brown background show?

A   Primary roads

B   Minor roads

C   Tourist directions

D   Major roads

Answers

Question 12

C - When driving at higher speeds, there is more stress on the tyres, therefore inflating them to a higher pressure will give them more support over a long journey. This is particularly important when you are also carrying a heavy load. Check your vehicle handbook for guidance.

Question 13

A - All driving examiners are trained to assess candidates who have special needs. The physical disability should be declared when the test is applied for. This is to allow extra time for the

- examiner to discuss and understand how the disability affects the candidate's ability to control the vehicle
- subsequent paperwork.

The driving test itself will be of the same duration and assessed to the same uniform standard as all regular practical driving tests.

Question 14

C - Signs with a brown background give directions to places of interest. They're often seen on a motorway, directing you along the easiest route to the attraction.

Question 15 *

During a driving test, when the examiner gives the signal to carry out an emergency stop, what's the first thing the candidate should do?

A   Look in the mirrors

B   Put the clutch pedal down

C   Move over towards the kerb

D   Brake firmly and promptly

Question 16 *

You want to turn right from a one-way street. Where should you position your car?

A   Well to the right of the road

B   Well to the left of the road

C   Just left of the road centre

D   It doesn't matter in a one-way street

Question 17 *

You have a hand held mobile phone in your vehicle. What should you do to make a call whilst in traffic?

A   Dial the number while the handset is in the cradle

B   Find a safe place to stop before you pick the phone up

C   Wait until you're stationary at traffic lights

D   Pull up on double yellow lines with your hazard lights on

Answers

Question 15

D - It is the examiner's responsibility to make sure that there is nothing behind the car before giving the signal. The candidate only needs to be concerned with keeping control of the car while braking promptly and firmly to a stop.

Question 16

A - In a one-way street you should position on the right hand side, and take up this position as soon as you can to make sure that no-one can come up on the outside of you.

Question 17

B - It is unsafe and against the law to use a hand held phone while driving, even when stationary in traffic queues. You MUST find a safe place to pull over and stop before using it and that does not include double yellow lines which indicate that waiting restrictions apply.

Question 18 *

It is a bright and sunny day. You are about to drive through a tunnel. What should you do before you enter it?

A   Turn off the radio

B   Take of your sunglasses

C   Switch off your mobile phone

D   Turn on the demisters

Question 19 *

Your pupil is driving towards a right-hand bend. Why should you advise them to keep well to the left?

A   To allow faster traffic to overtake

B   To improve your view of the road

C   To overcome the effect of the road's camber

D   To be positioned safely if you skid

Question 20

Normally, how far apart are emergency telephones on a motorway?

A   ½ a mile

B   1 mile

C   2 miles

D   3 miles

Answers

Question 18

B - Tunnels can be quite dark; you need to be able to see properly so if you are wearing sunglasses they should be removed until you reach the end.

Question 19

B - By taking a position well to the left as you enter a right-hand bend, you'll improve your view around the corner. This will help you to see any hazards as soon as possible. Positioning well to the left also reduces the risk of collision with an oncoming vehicle that may have drifted over the centre line.

Question 20

B - Emergency telephones on the motorway are connected to control centres, where the operator can identify your location from the telephone you're using. To help you locate an emergency telephone, marker posts are situated at 100 metre intervals. These marker posts have arrows directing you to the nearest telephone. Emergency telephones are spaced at 1 mile intervals.

Question 21

Where would you see this sign?

A　At the end of a dual carriageway

B　At a road narrowing

C　At the end of a one-way street

D　At the beginning of a contra-flow system

Question 22

There are no speed-limit signs on the road. In England, Scotland and Northern Ireland how is a 30 mph limit generally indicated?

A　By double or single yellow lines

B　By hazard warning lines

C　By pedestrian islands

D　By street lighting

Answers

Question 21

B - This sign will be used where the road narrows, often as a result of traffic calming measures. When you see this you should give way to oncoming traffic.

Question 22

D - In England, Scotland and Northern Ireland, there's a 30 mph speed limit where there are street lights unless signs show another limit. In Wales, street lights indicate the limit is 20 mph unless signs show otherwise.

Question 23 *

What do these road markings mean?

A   Keep two chevrons apart

B   One way street

C   Do not cross

D   Speed humps

Question 24

What will a new driver have to do if they accrue six or more penalty points on their licence within the first two years after passing their first driving test?

A   Retake the practical test only

B   Retake the theory test only

C   Retake both the theory and practical tests

D   Reapply for a full licence immediately

Answers

Question 23

C - These markings are seen on a motorway separating lanes, normally where a slip road joins the motorway or where motorways separate. You MUST not cross these where the border is solid except in an unavoidable emergency.

Question 24

C - If the number of points on a new driver's licence (including any points gained as a learner) reaches six or more within two years of passing their first practical driving test, their licence will be revoked. To regain a full driving licence, both the theory and practical tests will have to be retaken.

Question 25

Where should you not use a breakdown warning triangle?

A   On a dual carriageway

B   On a single-track road

C   On a narrow country road

D   On a motorway

Question 26

You see a pedestrian carrying a white stick with a red band. What does this tell you?

A   The person is physically disabled

B   The person is a pensioner

C   The person has memory problems

D   The person is deaf and blind

Answers

Question 25

D - If your vehicle breaks down, be aware of the danger to, and from, other traffic. Get your vehicle off the road if possible. Use a warning triangle to alert other road users to the obstruction but NOT when you're on a motorway. The risk of walking along the hard shoulder to place the triangle is too great.

Question 26

D - If someone is deaf as well as blind, they may be carrying a white stick with a red reflective band. You can't know whether a pedestrian is deaf. Don't assume that everyone can hear you approaching.

Question 27 *

You are waiting to turn right from a side road. There is a vehicle approaching from the right which is signalling to turn left. What advice should you give to your pupil?

A   To be confident and pull out without delay

B   To make sure the driver is going to turn before pulling out

C   To start edging forward ready to go

D   To apply the parking brake and select neutral while waiting

Question 28

Your pupil's knowledge and driving competence improve. What should happen to the level of instructor involvement?

A   It should remain the same

B   It should increase

C   It should decrease

D   It should finish

Question 29

Overall stopping distance is made up of thinking distance and braking distance. You are on a good, dry road surface, with good brakes and tyres. What is the typical braking distance from 50 mph?

A   14 metres (46 feet)

B   24 metres (80 feet)

C   38 metres (125 feet)

D   55 metres (180 feet)

Answers

Question 27

B - It is quite common for drivers to forget to cancel their signals and this alone is no guarantee that they intend to turn. You should advise your pupil to be ready to go, but to make certain that the other driver is turning before they set off.

Question 28

C - Detailed instruction should decrease as the pupil's ability increases. An instructor shouldn't be controlling the pupil all of the time. This takes the initiative away from them and could be considered over-instruction.

Question 29

C - Be aware that this is just the braking distance. You need to add the thinking distance to this to give the overall stopping distance. At 50 mph, the typical thinking distance will be 15 metres (50 feet), plus a braking distance of 38 metres (125 feet), giving an overall stopping distance of 53 metres (175 feet). The stopping distance could be greater than this, depending on your attention and response to any hazards. These figures are a general guide.

Question 30 *

Which of the following documents may the police ask you to produce after you have been involved in a road incident?

A Your driving licence

B Your ADI licence

C Your V5C document

D Your vehicle road tax receipt

Question 31 *

What advice should you give your pupil about changing lanes at speed?

A That they should use mirrors and turn to check over their right shoulder

B That they should use all mirrors in good time and signal if necessary

C That they only need to use the exterior mirror before signalling

D That they should slow down before checking their mirrors and signalling

Question 32

Your vehicle catches fire while driving through a tunnel. It is still driveable. What should you do?

A Drive it out of the tunnel if you can do so

B Leave it where it is, with the engine running

C Stop, and wait for help to arrive

D Pull up, then walk to an emergency telephone

Answers

Question 30

A - You must stop if you've been involved in a collision which results in injury or damage. The police may ask to see your driving licence and insurance details at the time or later at a police station.

Question 31

B - If someone directly behind is about to move out to pass you, they may not be visible if only the exterior mirror is used. On no account should you teach someone to turn to look over their shoulder, they may lose control of the wheel and may not react in time to what is in front of them.

Question 32

A - If it's possible, and you can do so without causing further danger, it may be safer to drive a vehicle that's on fire out of a tunnel. The greatest danger in a tunnel fire is smoke and suffocation.

Question 33

You begin to suffer from ill health which affects your driving. What must you do?

A   Ask your doctor for an exemption certificate

B   Reduce your working hours

C   Inform the licensing authority

D   Inform your local police station

Question 34

When is it acceptable for a passenger to travel in a car without wearing a seat belt?

A   When they are exempt for medical reasons

B   When they are sitting in the rear seat

C   When they are under 1.5 metres (5 feet) in height

D   When they are under 14 years old

Question 35

When should you assess a learner driver's progress?

A   Continuously, using dialogue and feedback

B   When an improvement has been made

C   At the end of the course of lessons

D   When the pupil has learnt as much as they can at that time

Answers

Question 33

C - You must tell DVLA (or DVA in Northern Ireland) if your health is likely to affect your ability to drive. The licensing authority will investigate your situation and then make a decision on whether or not to take away your licence.

Question 34

A - Where fitted, seat belts must be worn. It's the driver's responsibility to ensure that children under 14 years old wear a seat belt or use a suitable child restraint. Passengers aged 14 or over are responsible for wearing their seat belt. Exceptions to this law are made for people who hold a medical exemption certificate.

Question 35

A - In client-centred learning, there should be lots of opportunities for you to observe how your pupil's learning is going. You should provide frequent feedback on their progress, based on these observations, and talk to your pupil about how they view their progress. Then you can adjust the lesson content to meet your pupil's learning needs.

Question 36

What does this sign mean?

A   Level crossing with gate or barrier

B   Gated road ahead

C   Farm entrance ahead

D   Cattle grid ahead

Question 37

What does a differential do when a car is cornering?

A   It allows the driven wheels to turn at the same speed

B   It allows the outer driven wheel to turn more slowly than the inner wheel

C   It allows the driven wheels to rotate in opposite directions

D   It allows the inner driven wheel to turn more slowly than the outer wheel

Answers

Question 36

A - Some crossings have gates but no attendant or signals. You should stop, look both ways, listen and make sure that no train is approaching. If there's a telephone, contact the signal operator to make sure it's safe to cross.

Question 37

D - The differential mechanism enables the inside wheel to turn at a slower rate than the outer wheel when the car is being driven on a curve. This helps both stability and grip while the car is cornering or turning.

Question 38

What does this sign mean?

A No entry for traffic turning left

B No through road on the left

C Turn left for ferry terminal

D Turn left for parking area

Question 39 *

What would these road markings be used to highlight?

A A pedestrianised area

B A pelican crossing

C A level crossing

D A hump in the road surface

Answers

Question 38

B - This sign shows you that you can't get through to another route by turning left at the junction ahead.

Question 39

D - Changes in road level aren't always easily seen. White triangles painted on the road surface give you an indication of where there are road humps.

Question 40

Which of these is a hazard warning line?

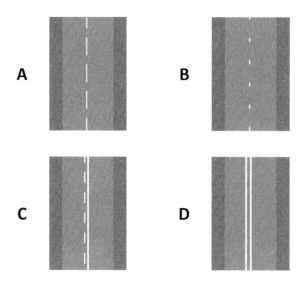

A

B

C

D

Question 41

You're towing a small trailer on a busy three-lane motorway. All lanes are open. Which of these is correct?

A   You must have a stabiliser fitted

B   You must not exceed 50 mph

C   You must not overtake

D   You may only use the left-hand and centre lanes

Answers

Question 40

A - You need to know the difference between the normal centre line and a hazard warning line. If there's a hazard ahead, the markings are longer and the gaps shorter. This gives you advance warning of an unspecified hazard.

Question 41

D - The motorway regulations for towing a trailer state that you mustn't
- use the right-hand lane of a three-lane motorway unless directed to do so (for example, at roadworks or due to a lane closure)
- exceed 60 mph.

Question 42 *

You're approaching a set of traffic lights. They have been on green for quite a while. What advice should you give your pupil?

A   Pick up speed before they change

B   Check the mirrors and prepare to stop

C   Change into a lower gear

D   Maintain a steady speed

Question 43 *

A cover note will generally last for 30 to 60 days. What is a cover note?

A   A temporary MOT certificate

B   A temporary test pass certificate

C   A temporary licence to drive

D   A temporary certificate of insurance

Question 44 *

When is a learner driver allowed to drive on a motorway?

A   Only if they are in a dual-controlled car with an instructor

B   When they have a qualified driver alongside them

C   Only after passing their driving test

D   When they remove the 'L' plates from their car

Answers

Question 42

B - Lights which have green for a long time are possibly about to change. You should teach your pupil to check their mirrors, ease off the gas and be ready to stop in case they do.

Question 43

D - A cover note is an insurance policy which will give short term cover. It will usually only last until the full insurance policy documents are prepared and sent out. The length of time it remains valid will depend on the company that issued it.

Question 44

A - Before June 2018 learner drivers were not allowed on motorways. From that date they can practise on motorways providing that they are with an approved driving instructor in a car with dual brakes.

Question 45

You've broken down on a two-way road. You have a warning triangle. At least how far from your vehicle should you place the warning triangle?

A   100 metres (328 feet)

B   25 metres (82 feet)

C   45 metres (147 feet)

D   5 metres (16 feet)

Question 46

What can be established through an appropriate use of open questions during driving lessons?

A   The pupil's level of practical and theoretical knowledge

B   The pupil's attitude and motivation when learning to drive

C   The pupil's degree of aptitude and psychomotor skills

D   If the ADI and the pupil have any interests in common

Answers

Question 45

C - Advance warning triangles fold flat and don't take up much room. Use one to warn other road users if your vehicle has broken down or if there has been an incident. Place it at least 45 metres (147 feet) behind your vehicle (or the incident), on the same side of the road or verge. Place it further back if the scene is hidden by, for example, a bend, hill or dip in the road. Don't use warning triangles on motorways.

Question 46

B - The decisions we make when driving are shaped by our attitude and motivation. But we're not always aware of these. Open questions can be used to explore these issues without making the pupil defensive. You can then work with the pupil to address any unhelpful attitudes.

Question 47

Who's responsible for making sure that a vehicle isn't overloaded?

A   The driver of the vehicle

B   The licensing authority

C   The owner of the items being carried

D   The person who loaded the vehicle

Question 48

You're driving down a long, steep hill. You suddenly notice that your brakes aren't working as well as normal. What's the usual cause of this?

A   Air in the brake fluid

B   Badly adjusted brakes

C   Oil on the brakes

D   The brakes overheating

Answers

Question 47

A - Carrying heavy loads will affect control and the vehicle's handling characteristics. If the vehicle you're driving is overloaded, you will be held responsible.

Question 48

D - Continuous use of the brakes can cause them to start overheating. This is more likely to happen on vehicles fitted with drum brakes, but it can apply to disc brakes as well. Using a lower gear will assist the braking and help you to keep control of your vehicle.

Question 49

Why are these yellow lines painted across the road?

A To help you choose the correct lane

B To help you keep the correct separation distance

C To make you aware of your speed

D To tell you the distance to the roundabout

Question 50 *

You see this sign on a motorway, what is it telling you?

A You should move to the lane on your left

B You must not move into the left hand lane

C You must leave the motorway at the next exit

D You should move across to the hard shoulder

Answers

Question 49

C - These lines are often found on the approach to a roundabout or a dangerous junction. They give you extra warning to adjust your speed. Look well ahead and do this in good time.

Question 50

A - Overhead signs on motorways will give instructions such as temporary speed limits and lane closures. This sign tells you to move into the next lane on your left.

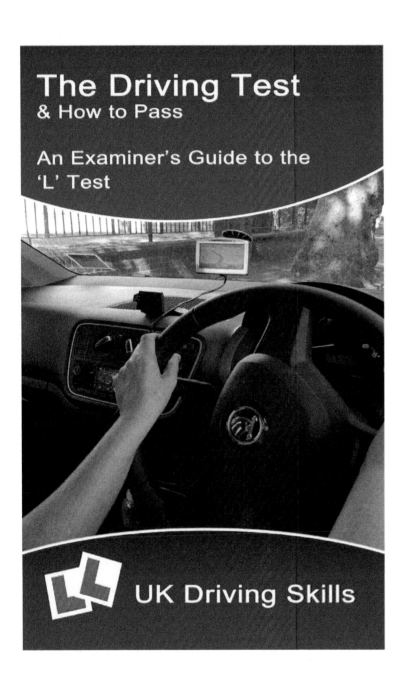

The Driving Test
& How to Pass

An Examiner's Guide to the 'L' Test

UK Driving Skills

Test Five

Question 1

When should anti-freeze be used in the cooling system?

A In winter only

B In autumn and winter

C Only when it is icy

D All year round

Question 2 *

What should you teach your pupils to do before pulling up in a clear space at the side of the road?

A Select third gear before braking

B Stay in the current gear

C Change down through all the gears

D Select neutral before braking

Question 3

On a vehicle, where would you find a catalytic converter?

A On the exhaust system

B In the fuel tank

C On the cooling system

D In the air filter

Answers

Question 1

D - Today, all water-cooled engines use a mixture of water and anti-freeze to make up the coolant. As well as helping to keep the engine at its correct operating temperature, the anti-freeze acts as a corrosion inhibitor to prolong the life of the cooling system.

Question 2

A - There should be no need to change down before pulling up into a clear space. The car can be stopped in any gear with the clutch being disengaged just before coming to rest. It is not a fault to change into a lower gear, but generally this should only be done when speed needs to be reduced more in order to steer into a more confined space.

Question 3

A - Although carbon dioxide is still produced, a catalytic converter fitted to the exhaust system reduces the toxic and polluting gases by up to 90%.

Question 4

You're driving downhill. How will this affect your vehicle?

A   It will need more engine power

B   It will take longer to stop

C   It will increase fuel consumption

D   It will be easier to change direction

Question 5 *

You're about to move from the right-hand lane of a motorway back into the centre lane after overtaking. Why should you consider signalling left before doing so?

A   Because it's always necessary to signal left after overtaking

B   To let the driver you have passed know that you are moving in

C   In case drivers ahead are about to leave the motorway

D   In case drivers in the left-hand lane are about to move out

Answers

Question 4

B - When driving downhill, gravity will cause the vehicle to increase speed. More braking effort will be required, and stopping distances will increase.

Question 5

D - Moving back to the left after overtaking is what you're supposed to do, and what other drivers expect you to do. It should not normally need a signal to overstate the obvious. On a road with three lanes however, as you're about to move back to the middle lane, drivers in the left could also be thinking about moving into that lane to overtake vehicles ahead of them. It is these drivers who may need a signal from you.

Question 6

What does this motorway sign mean?

A   You're approaching a long downhill slope

B   You're approaching a long uphill slope

C   You're approaching a 'lorries only' lane

D   You're approaching a service area

Question 7 *

You're planning to overtake on a single carriageway road. What do you need to be aware of?

A   That there may be junctions ahead that you can't see

B   That you need to keep close to the other vehicle before pulling out

C   That the other driver may decide to wave you past

D   That you mustn't exceed the speed limit by more than 10mph

Answers

Question 6

B - The term 'crawler lane' doesn't mean the lane is only for extremely slow vehicles. It's advising you of an extra lane on the left. Crawler lanes are usually built on sections of road where the length of the gradient is such that some large vehicles will be slowed to the point where they become a hazard for other road users.

Question 7

A - Before overtaking, you need to make sure it's safe to carry out the manoeuvre. As part of your check, look well ahead for road junctions. You shouldn't overtake as you approach a road junction, because if a vehicle emerges you could risk a collision.

Question 8 *

After using the right-hand lane of a motorway to overtake, when would it be wise to stay in that lane instead of moving promptly back to the middle lane?

A When you want to continue driving at a higher speed

B When there is nothing following close behind you

C When the driver you have passed flashes their lights

D When vehicles are bunching up together in the left-hand lane

Question 9

You're at a road junction, turning into a minor road. What should you do if there are pedestrians crossing the minor road?

A Stop and wave the pedestrians across

B Sound your horn to let the pedestrians know that you're there

C Give way to the pedestrians who are already crossing

D Carry on; the pedestrians should give way to you

Question 10 *

Why is it a good idea to switch to a local radio station before entering a tunnel?

A Because the local radio content will be better

B Because national radio signals will be lost

C Because it will be compatible with your sat nav

D Because it may give you information about any problems ahead

Answers

Question 8

D - After overtaking you should normally move back to the lane on your left as soon as it's safe to do so. If you see vehicles bunching up in the left-hand lane however; this could be a sign that one or more of them may be about to pull out to overtake. In this situation you should stay in the right-hand lane until you're sure it's safe to move back to your left.

Question 9

C - Always look into the road you're entering. If pedestrians are already crossing, be considerate and give way to them. Don't wave or signal them to hurry; they have priority here.

Question 10

D - On the approach to many tunnels, a board will indicate a local channel or radio frequency that you should tune into. This should give a warning of any incident or congestion in the tunnel ahead. Severe loss of life has occurred in tunnel fires. Getting advance warning of any problems ahead will help you to take appropriate action in good time.

Question 11

What should you do if a front tyre bursts while you're driving on a motorway?

A   Loosen your grip on the steering wheel

B   Brake firmly to a stop

C   Hold the steering wheel firmly

D   Drive to the next service area

Question 12 *

What should you do when approaching a sharp bend on an icy road?

A   Take the car out of gear to avoid wheel-spin

B   Brake firmly to activate the ABS system

C   Keep braking gently all the way through the bend

D   Slow down well before reaching the bend

Question 13

You're turning right at a crossroads. An oncoming driver is also turning right. What's the advantage of turning behind the oncoming vehicle?

A   You'll use less fuel because you can stay in a higher gear

B   You'll have more time to make the turn

C   You'll have a clearer view of any approaching traffic

D   You'll be able to turn without stopping

Answers

Question 11

C - A front tyre bursting will seriously reduce your control of the vehicle. Keep calm and resist the temptation to brake hard or swerve. Hold the steering wheel firmly and try to get the vehicle onto the hard shoulder while allowing it to slow down gradually. Stop as far to the left as possible and switch on your hazard warning lights.

Question 12

D - Harsh use of the accelerator, brakes or steering is likely to lead to skidding, especially on slippery surfaces. Avoid steering and braking at the same time. In icy conditions it's very important that you constantly assess what's ahead, so that you can take appropriate action in plenty of time.

Question 13

C - When turning right at a crossroads where oncoming traffic is also turning right, it's generally safer to turn behind the approaching vehicle. This allows you a clear view of approaching traffic and is called 'turning offside to offside'. However, some junctions, usually controlled by traffic-light filters - are marked for vehicles to turn nearside to nearside and this is much more commonly done on busy roads.

Question 14

You're testing your suspension. You notice that your vehicle keeps bouncing when you press down on the front wing. What does this mean?

A   Worn tyres

B   Tyres under-inflated

C   Steering wheel not located centrally

D   Worn shock absorbers

Question 15

Which of the following may help to deter a thief from stealing your car?

A   Parking near to other vehicles for security

B   Fitting tinted windows to make it difficult to see inside

C   Using a 'No valuables left inside' sticker on the window

D   Etching the registration number on the windows

Question 16

You have too much oil in your engine. What could this cause?

A   Oil leaks

B   Low oil pressure

C   Engine overheating

D   Carburettor damage

Answers

Question 14

D - If you find that your vehicle bounces as you drive around a corner or bend in the road, the shock absorbers might be worn. Press down on the front wing and, if the vehicle continues to bounce, take it to be checked by a qualified mechanic.

Question 15

D - Having your car registration number etched on all your windows is a cheap and effective way to deter professional car thieves. This would mean that they would have to go to the expense of replacing all the glass if they tried to sell it on.

Question 16

A - Too much oil in the engine will create excess pressure and could damage engine seals and cause oil leaks. Any excess oil should be drained off.

Question 17

How should you overtake a long, slow-moving vehicle on a busy road?

A   Follow it closely and keep moving out to see the road ahead

B   Edge out so that the oncoming traffic gives way

C   Stay behind until the driver waves you past

D   Keep well back until you can see that it's clear

Question 18 *

What is the best way to drive your vehicle through a ford?

A   Drive through slowly in low gear

B   Drive through quickly in low gear

C   Drive through slowly in high gear

D   Drive through quickly in high gear

Answers

Question 17

D - When you're following a long vehicle, stay well back so that you can get a better view of the road ahead. The closer you get, the less you'll be able to see of the road. Be patient and don't take a gamble. Only overtake when you're certain that you can complete the manoeuvre safely.

Question 18

A - In normal conditions, a ford can be crossed quite safely by driving through it slowly. You need to prevent water from entering through the exhaust by keeping the 'revs' high in a low gear. This can be helped by slipping the clutch if necessary to keep revs high but speed low.

Question 19 *

You're travelling in the left-hand lane of a motorway. What should you do when there are vehicles about to join from the slip road just ahead of you?

A   Speed up to get past them

B   Maintain a steady speed

C   Quickly brake to give way to them

D   Move to another lane if you can

Question 20 *

A cycle lane is marked by a solid white line. What does this mean?

A   Drivers can use it only when parking

B   Drivers must not use that lane at any time

C   Drivers may use the lane at any time

D   Drivers may only use the lane at certain times

Question 21 *

You're driving at night with your headlights on full beam. A vehicle is about to overtake you. When should you dip your lights?

A   Shortly after the vehicle has passed you

B   You should dip them immediately

C   Only if the other driver dips their headlights

D   As soon as the vehicle is about to pass you

Answers

Question 19

D - Plan well ahead when approaching a slip road. If you see traffic joining the motorway, move to another lane if it's safe to do so. This can help the flow of traffic joining the motorway, especially at peak times. You must be careful however not to change lanes unsafely and cause problems for other drivers behind you.

Question 20

B - Cycle lanes which are marked with a continuous solid white line are for cyclists only. You must not drive or ride a motorcycle along it any time. Nor should you park within this area.

Question 21

D - Leaving them on full beam for a few moments as they are pulling out will light the way ahead, but dip your lights as soon as the driver is about to pass you.

Question 22

There's been a collision. A driver is suffering from shock. What should you do?

A   Give them a drink

B   Ask who caused the incident

C   Leave them alone to recover

D   Try to reassure them

Question 23 *

Where should you never consider overtaking a cyclist?

A   On a left-hand bend

B   Just before you turn right

C   Just before you turn left

D   On a right-hand bend

Question 24

What should you do when you're overtaking at night?

A   Wait until a bend so that you can see oncoming headlights

B   Flash your lights before moving out

C   Put your headlights on full beam

D   Beware of bends in the road ahead

Answers

Question 22

D - A casualty suffering from shock may have injuries that aren't immediately obvious. Call the emergency services, then stay with the person in shock, offering reassurance until the experts arrive.

Question 23

C - If there is a cyclist just ahead of you as you approach a junction you should never overtake just before turning left. Keep a safe distance behind and allow the rider to pass the junction before you turn.

Even when you're turning right you still need to exercise caution. You may be able to overtake safely if the road is wide enough but always be aware that the rider may also decide to turn right. Hold back if you are in any doubt.

Question 24

D - Don't overtake if there's a possibility of a road junction, bend or brow of a bridge or hill ahead. There are many hazards that are difficult to see in the dark. Only overtake if you're certain that the road ahead is clear. Don't take a chance.

Question 25 *

When is it against the law to sound your vehicle's horn in a built up area?

A   Between 11.30 pm and 7.00 am

B   Between midnight and 8 am

C   At any time when you're stationary

D   At any time during the night

Question 26

What fault would you suspect if the footbrake on your car starts to feel spongy?

A   The wrong brake pads are fitted

B   The brake pads are worn

C   The hydraulic system contains air

D   The brake discs are worn

Question 27

What should you check when you're leaving a motorway after travelling at speed for some time?

A   The speedometer

B   The fuel level

C   The engine temperature

D   The brakes

Answers

Question 25

A - You mustn't sound your horn in a built-up area between 11.30 pm and 7.00 am in order to avoid disturbing people who may be sleeping.

When stationary, although you may sound your horn to warn someone else of danger, it should not be used in any other situation when stationary even during the day.

Question 26

C - If air gets into the hydraulic system, the brake pedal will feel spongy. When you press it, the air is compressed, causing the pedal to move further than normal. As a result, braking efficiency is reduced. Have the system checked by a qualified mechanic: brake faults are too important to be ignored.

Question 27

A - After leaving a motorway or when using a link road between motorways, your speed may be higher than you realise: 50 mph may feel like 30 mph. Check the speedometer and adjust your speed accordingly.

Question 28

While driving at night, you see a pedestrian ahead. What does it mean if they're wearing reflective clothing and carrying a red light?

A   You're approaching men at work

B   You're approaching an incident blackspot

C   You're approaching slow-moving vehicles

D   You're approaching an organised walk

Question 29

Over what distance are you allowed to reverse?

A   No further than is necessary

B   No more than the length of your vehicle

C   As far as it takes to reverse around a corner

D   The length of a residential street

Question 30 *

Where are motorcyclists and cyclists particularly vulnerable?

A   At junctions

B   On dual carriageways

C   On country roads

D   In urban areas

Answers

Question 28

D - Pedestrians who are part of an organised walk using the road at night should wear bright or reflective clothing. The walker in front should display a white light, while the one at the back should display a red light. Be particularly careful, slow down and give the walkers plenty of room.

Question 29

A - You mustn't reverse further than is absolutely necessary. You may decide to turn your vehicle around by reversing into an opening or side road. When you reverse, always look all around you, and watch for pedestrians. Never reverse from a side road into a main road.

Question 30

A - Motorcyclists and cyclists who may be nearer to the kerb than other vehicles can be harder to see when you're emerging from a junction. Their relatively smaller size means that they can also be hidden from view by obstructions such as parked cars and 'street furniture'.

Question 31

What's the maximum fine for driving without insurance?

A £500

B Unlimited

C £1000

D £5000

Question 32 *

Your pupil is worried that the examiner not know when they're using the mirrors during their driving test. What advice should you give them?

A Tell them to exaggerate their head movements

B Tell them to continue using their mirrors normally

C Tell them to adjust the mirrors so that they have to move their head

D Tell them to look in mirrors for longer and more often

Question 33

What does it mean if the signs at a bus lane show no times of operation?

A The lane isn't in operation

B The lane is only in operation at peak times

C The lane is only in operation in daylight hours

D The lane is in operation 24 hours a day

Answers

Question 31

B - It's a serious offence to drive without insurance. As well as an unlimited fine, you may be disqualified or given penalty points.

Question 32

B - Examiners are trained to detect the proper use of mirrors and your pupils should not use them any differently to the way they do during driving lessons. What you need to impress on your pupils is that just looking is not enough. They need to look early enough, judge what may happen, and to act safely and sensibly on what they see.

Question 33

D - Bus lane signs show the vehicles allowed to use the lane and also its times of operation. Where no times are shown, the bus lane is in operation 24 hours a day.

Question 34

You want to put a rear-facing baby seat on the front passenger seat, which is protected by a frontal airbag. What must you do before setting off?

A   Turn the seat to face sideways

B   Deactivate the airbag

C   Make sure the passenger door is locked

D   Put the child in an adult seat belt

Question 35 *

You're about to reverse out of a supermarket parking bay. What do you need to be particularly aware of?

A   Shopping trolleys

B   Bollards and barriers

C   Small children

D   Other drivers

Question 36

Daytime visibility is poor and misty but not seriously reduced. Which lights should you switch on?

A   Main beam headlights

B   Front fog lights

C   Dipped headlights

D   Rear fog lights

Answers

Question 34

B - It's illegal to fit a rear-facing baby seat into a passenger seat protected by an active frontal airbag. If the airbag activates, it could cause serious injury or even death to the child. You must secure it in a different seat or deactivate the relevant airbag. Follow the manufacturer's advice when fitting a baby seat.

Question 35

C - Small children can be difficult to see when you're reversing especially if they are close to the rear of your car. Always look around thoroughly and constantly and NEVER rely on mirrors alone.

Question 36

C - Only use your fog lights when visibility is seriously reduced. Use dipped headlights in poor conditions because this helps other road users to see you without the risk of causing dazzle.

Question 37

Where would you see a contraflow bus and cycle lane?

A   On a dual carriageway

B   On a roundabout

C   On an urban motorway

D   On a one-way street

Question 38

What does this sign mean?

A   Danger ahead

B   Tunnel ahead

C   Slippery road

D   Flood water

Answers

Question 37

D - The traffic permitted to use a contraflow lane travels in the opposite direction to traffic in the other lanes on the road.

Question 38

A - This sign is not used for any specific situation but is there to warn you of danger. You will often see it with an information plate below describing the nature of the hazard.

Question 39 *

Your pupil has stalled in the middle of a level crossing and can't restart the engine. The warning bells start to ring. What should you do?

A   Swap seats and try to start the engine yourself

B   Get out of the car and clear of the crossing

C   Let them carry on trying to restart the engine

D   Push the vehicle clear of the crossing

Question 40

You're in collision with another moving vehicle. Someone is injured and your vehicle is damaged. What information should you find out?

A   Whether the other driver is licensed to drive

B   The other driver's name, address and telephone number

C   The destination of the other driver

D   The occupation of the other driver

Question 41

You're planning a long journey. Do you need to plan rest stops?

A   Yes, you should plan to stop every half an hour

B   No, you'll be less tired if you get there as soon as possible

C   Yes, regular stops help concentration

D   Yes, but only in very bad weather conditions

Answers

Question 39

B - If they can't restart the engine before the warning bells ring, leave the vehicle and get yourselves out of the car and well clear of the crossing. Use the phone if there is one to alert the signal operator of the danger.

Question 40

B - Try to keep calm and don't rush. Make sure that you've shared all the relevant details with the other driver before you leave the scene. If possible, take pictures and note the positions of all the vehicles involved.

Question 41

C - Try to plan your journey so that you can take rest stops. It's recommended that you take a break of at least 15 minutes after every two hours of driving. This should help to maintain your concentration.

Question 42 *

Your car has a reversing camera. How should your pupils make use of this during a driving test?

A   They can use it in place of observation around the car

B   They can use it in addition to taking observation around the car

C   They cannot use the camera at any time when reversing

D   They can only use it when the car is stationary

Question 43

Traffic officers operate on motorways and some primary routes in England. What are they authorised to do?

A   Stop and arrest drivers who break the law

B   Repair broken-down vehicles on the motorway

C   Stop and direct anyone on a motorway

D   Issue fixed penalty notices

Answers

Question 42

B - Reversing cameras are useful aids but they don't always give a full field of vision and the view is often distorted. They can be used to aid observation when reversing, but at no time should the pupil neglect to take proper observation all around the car.

Question 43

C - Traffic officers don't have enforcement powers but are able to stop and direct people on motorways and some 'A' class roads. They only operate in England and work in partnership with the police at incidents, providing a highly trained and visible service. They're recognised by an orange-and-yellow jacket and their vehicle has yellow-and-black markings.

Question 44

What does this sign mean?

A   Minimum speed 30 mph

B   End of minimum speed

C   End of maximum speed

D   Maximum speed 30 mph

Question 45

In which of these situations should you avoid overtaking?

A   Just after a bend

B   In a one-way street

C   On a 30 mph road

D   Approaching a dip in the road

Answers

Question 44

C - The red slash through the sign indicates that the restriction has ended. In this case, the restriction was a minimum speed limit of 30 mph.

Question 45

D - Oncoming vehicles or other hazards can be hidden from view by dips in the road. If you can't see into the dip, wait until you have a clear view and can see that it's safe before starting to overtake.

Question 46

An injured person has been placed in the recovery position. They're unconscious but breathing normally. What else should be done?

A   Check their airway remains open

B   Press firmly between their shoulders

C   Place their arms by their side

D   Turn them over every few minutes

Question 47

You're driving in falling snow. What should you do if your wipers aren't clearing the windscreen?

A   Set the windscreen demister to cool

B   Use the windscreen washers

C   Partly open the front windows

D   Be prepared to clear the windscreen by hand

Question 48

Where should the head restraint be positioned for it to be most effective?

A   At least as high as the shoulders

B   At least as high as the eyes or top of the ears

C   In the lowest position and pointing forwards

D   In the highest position and tilted backwards

Answers

Question 46

A - After a casualty has been placed in the recovery position, make sure their airway remains open and monitor their condition until medical help arrives. Where possible, don't move a casualty unless there's further danger.

Question 47

D - Before you set off, you should make sure that you can see clearly through all the windows. Don't just rely on the wipers, as this will leave dangerous blind spots. If you need to, pull up safely and clear the windows by hand.

Question 48

B - An incorrectly adjusted head restraint will offer reduced protection against whiplash injury. When adjusting the head restraint, set it so that it's at least as high as the eyes or top of the ears.

Question 49 *

You're on a driving lesson when your mobile phone rings. What action should you take?

A   Ignore it. Deal with the call once the driving lesson has finished

B   It's okay to pick the phone up as you're not the one doing the driving

C   You can take the call but only if you're using hands free

D   Ask the pupil if they're happy for you to answer the phone

Question 50 *

What's the best way to drive a car through a bend in the road?

A   With continuous pressure on the footbrake

B   With even steady pressure on the accelerator

C   With the clutch pedal fully pressed down

D   With your feet fully away from the pedals

Answers

Question 49

A - Not only is it against the law for drivers to use hand-held mobile phones or other electronic devices (except when safely and legally parked), it's also against the law for an accompanying driver to use any such device whilst supervising a learner driver.

Even if you're parked up safely at the side of the road you should not interrupt the lesson flow by taking a personal call. Make sure yours is turned off or on silent while giving training to your learner.

Question 50

B - When taking a bend, the weight of the car is thrown onto the outside wheels of the car. Use of the brake will put extra load onto the front outside wheel and increases the risk of a skid. Using the accelerator lifts weight off the front of the car; therefore use of this pedal with just enough power to maintain a safe steady speed will give the best control when cornering.

Need More Practise?

Visit our website at UK Driving Skills and get access to around 800+ Theory Test Revision Questions, produced under licence from the DVSA.

Our interactive online tests each have 100 questions and are timed just like the real thing. You'll also be given a score at the end, plus an explanation of the answers.

Printed in Great Britain
by Amazon